YORK NOTES

General Editors: Professor A.N. Jeffares (*University of Stirling*) & Professor Suheil Bushrui (*American University of Beirut*)

R. C. Sherriff

JOURNEY'S END

Notes by Antony Kamm

MA (OXON)

**LONGMAN
YORK PRESS**

YORK PRESS
Immeuble Esseily, Place Riad Solh, Beirut.

LONGMAN GROUP LIMITED
Longman House, Burnt Mill,
Harlow, Essex CM20 2JE, England

First published 1990
Fifth impression 1995

ISBN 0-582-03825-1

Typeset by Gem Graphics, Trenance, Mawgan Porth, Cornwall
Produced by Longman Singapore Publishers Pte Ltd
Printed in Singapore

Contents

Part 1

Introduction

The British theatre in the 1920s

W. MacQueen Pope wrote of the period of the First World War of 1914–18, in his survey of the British theatre in the 1920s:

> There was little or no chance for serious drama or new thought. Those who stared into the face of death all day and night in France did not want that, they wanted glamour, girls and fun . . . . It was now a scramble to get as much as possible out of a public hungry for amusement and wishing to escape from reality. So, because it still dealt in illusion, the theatre held on – but not the theatre of pre-war days.*

And Allardyce Nicoll asserted that in about 1920 'the main force of realism [in the theatre] was then undoubtedly spent'.†

George Bernard Shaw (1856–1950), at the height of his dramatic powers and popularity, was now concerning himself with excursions into philosophy and dialectics, tinged with comedy, such as *Back to Methuselah* (1921), *Saint Joan* (1924), and *The Apple Cart* (1929), rather than with the social realism which had marked earlier plays such as *Mrs Warren's Profession* (written in 1893 but not performed until 1902), *Candida* (1895), and *Major Barbara* (1905). Only John Galsworthy (1867–1933) of really notable pre-war writers of realistic drama stuck to his guns, with *The Skin Game* (1920) and *Loyalties* (1922). New English dramatists who attempted to promote a resurgence of realism were largely confined to the now forgotten Clemence Dane (1885–1965) with *A Bill of Divorcement* (1921) and John van Druten (1901–57), whose *Young Woodley*, a study of adolescence, was produced in New York in 1925 but because of censorship not in Britain until 1928. It was Ireland which in Sean O'Casey (1880–1964) produced the most consistent and lasting writer of realistic drama of the period, with *The Shadow of a Gunman* (1923, London 1927), *Juno and the Paycock* (1924, London 1925), and *The Plough and the Stars* (1926). Paradoxically, O'Casey abandoned his homeland to settle in England in 1928 after his anti-war play about a footballer disabled in the First World War, *The*

*W. MacQueen Pope, *The Footlights Flickered*, Herbert Jenkins, London, 1959, pp. 23–4.
†Allardyce Nicoll, *British Drama*, Harrap, London, 4th edition 1947, p. 456.

Silver Tassie (see p. 43), was rejected by the Abbey Theatre in Dublin.

The radio was becoming a potent medium for entertaining the masses (and more critical listeners) in their own living-rooms, while the advent of the 'talking picture' with *The Jazz Singer* (1927) ensured that the illusion of live entertainment was now never far away from their homes. To combat these formidable and permanent threats, the London theatres and what was left of the once magnificent array of provincial theatres offered in the main musical comedies and farces, while W. Somerset Maugham (1874–1965) and Noël Coward (1899–1973), with his even lighter comedies, satisfied the newly-created demand for what G. S. Fraser in *The Modern Writer and His World* (Penguin, London, new edition 1970) referred to as 'suburban domestic drama'.

It was in this atmosphere that a clerk in an insurance office, who in his spare time wrote plays for his local rowing club to perform, produced the manuscript of a play based on his experiences at the front in the First World War. It was rejected by every theatrical management, but eventually put on for two performances only by the Stage Society. In spite of high praise, it languished once again, until an actor undertook to back it and manage it. Against all predictions, it ran for 594 consecutive performances in London, and 485 in New York. It was revived in London as recently as 1988, and performed on television in 1989. Its title is *Journey's End* and it was written by R. C. Sherriff.

Though he was not himself the product of a public school, that particularly English institution which traditionally has been the province of the upper and middle classes who could afford the privilege of paying for their sons' education, the public school ethos and public school values pervade the play. (That this is a naturalistic stance on the author's part is confirmed by his own experience, recorded below, of his first attempt to become an army officer.) These attitudes further highlight the fact that in the 1920s and up until the late 1950s, the legitimate theatre was largely an upper- and middle-class preserve.

The author

Robert Cedric Sherriff was born on 6 June 1896 in Hampton Wick, Surrey, and educated at Kingston Grammar School, after which he joined the London staff of Sun Insurance, for which his father had worked. In August 1914 he attempted to enlist in the army as an officer, with the following result.

'School?' inquired the adjutant. I told him and his face fell. He took up a printed list and searched through it. 'I'm sorry,' he said, 'but

'I'm afraid it isn't a public school.' I was mystified. I told him that my school, though small, was a very old and good one – founded, I said, by Queen Elizabeth in 1567. The adjutant was not impressed. He had lost all interest in me. 'I'm sorry,' he repeated. 'But our instructions are that all applicants for commissions must be selected from the recognized public schools and yours is not among them.' And that was that. It was a long, hard pull before I was at last accepted as an officer. Only then because the prodigious loss of officers in France had forced the authorities to lower their sights and accept young men outside the exclusive circle!*

He became a captain in the 9th Battalion, East Surrey Regiment, and was severely wounded at Passchendaele in 1917. After the war he returned to his former employer, working at the Trafalgar Square branch of the company, from which he administered insurance policies and claims on properties on the outskirts of west London. A keen oarsman, he joined the Kingston Rowing Club on the River Thames, and began to write plays for members of the club to perform as fund-raising activities towards the purchase of new boats. After four of these plays had also been submitted to the theatrical agent Curtis Brown, without success, he began a novel in his winter evenings.

The theme of the novel was the hero-worship of an older schoolboy, Dennis Stanhope, by Jimmy Raleigh, several years his junior. After their schooldays the roles were reversed. Jimmy became a successful businessman, who was now trying to help an unqualified and dis-illusioned Dennis to regain confidence in himself. The book was never finished but, with the post-school setting transferred to the western front during the First World War, the basic idea was reshaped into a play which he called *Journey's End*. On this occasion Curtis Brown were enthusiastic, while expressing warnings about prejudice on the part of London theatrical managements against war plays which proved only too accurate. *Journey's End* was finally, and with much misgiving, put on by the Stage Society in December 1928, and had its first public performance at the Apollo Theatre in London's West End the following month. Suddenly, Sherriff became one of the most talked-about English dramatists of the decade, and with several companies touring in the provinces, the production of the play in New York, Canada, Australia, and South Africa, and seventeen foreign-language versions playing in Europe, he was for a time, by his own account, earning royalties of £1000 per week, an enormous sum in the period before the Second World War.

If *Journey's End* was one turning point in Sherriff's life and career, the production of his next play, *Badger's Green* (1930), was another.

*Quoted in John Keegan, *The Face of Battle*, Penguin, London, new edition 1978, p. 224.

This pleasant comedy, with an English country atmosphere and a background of village cricket, about a reviled speculative builder who becomes a local hero, ran with difficulty only for a few weeks. Sherriff now determined on a new career as a schoolmaster. In 1931, aged thirty-five and slightly bald, he went up to New College, Oxford, to do a special course in history. After two terms, he accepted an invitation to go to Hollywood to write the film script for H. G. Wells's novel, *The Invisible Man*, returning in the autumn of 1932 to continue his studies. In spite of his age, he was regarded as a certainty to win a rowing Blue, but pleurisy, diagnosed actually during the trials, put paid to that, and the growing realisation that an honours degree was beyond him led to his abandoning university and the idea of teaching, though he remembered his stay at New College by endowing a scholarship there in 1937.

With the failure of another comedy, *Windfall* (1933), a reputation as a 'one-play man' seemed likely, but his long career as a writer had only just begun. He wrote the screen-plays for several Hollywood and British films, of which the most memorable are *Goodbye, Mr Chips* (from James Hilton's novel), *The Four Feathers* (from A. E. W. Mason's novel), *Quartet* (from four stories by W. Somerset Maugham), *Lady Hamilton* (starring Laurence Olivier and Vivien Leigh), *The Dam Busters*, and the classic 'Oscar' award-winning story of England in the Second World War, *Mrs Miniver*.

Before going up to Oxford, Sherriff had written a novel and submitted it to Victor Gollancz (1893–1967), who had published *Journey's End*. *The Fortnight in September* (1931) is an unpretentious, episodic story which follows the day-to-day activities of a suburban family on holiday at the Sussex seaside resort of Bognor. Somehow, it reached to people's hearts as in a different way *Journey's End* had. It sold 20,000 copies in its first month and was a best-seller in the U.S.A., too, besides being translated into many European languages. Of several other novels, the best is *The Wells of St Mary's* (1962), a black comedy about the discovery and local exploitation of a spring of water which has, or maybe only appears to have, recuperative properties.

With the actress Jeanne de Casalis he wrote *St Helena* (1935), a study of Napoleon's last years, which was the first modern play to be performed at the Old Vic theatre in London. He wrote nothing more for the stage for thirteen years. *Miss Mabel* (1948) is a mystery play which centres on the identity of two elderly ladies who are twins: which of the twins is the one still living, and has the survivor murdered her sister? *Home at Seven* (1950), another play about apparently ordinary people caught up in inexplicable events, with Ralph Richardson playing the part of a bank clerk who goes missing for twenty-four hours, was even more successful, and ran for 342 performances in the

West End. More satisfying to its author, however, was *The Long Sunset*, staged in Birmingham in 1955 but not in London until 1961. This historical drama of Britain at the end of the Roman occupation grew out of Sherriff's preoccupation with archaeology (just before the Second World War he bought, and excavated, his own Roman archaeological site at Angmering, near the Sussex coast), and his feeling for setting. Though originally written for the theatre, it was first performed on BBC radio, to an estimated audience of five million. In his selective but modest and engaging autobiographical study, Sherriff wrote of his saying goodbye to the theatre after the London failure of his last play, *A Shred of Evidence* (1960):

> I would rather have done so in a happier way, but I had a good deal more to be grateful for than sorry about. If the New Movement had started ten years earlier, when I had made my final effort at a come-back with *Miss Mabel*, they would have killed it stone-dead in a week: I should have been finished and done with, and *The Long Sunset*, *Home at Seven* and all the other plays that followed could never have been written. As it was, my plays, in London and the provinces, at home and abroad, had chalked up over five thousand performances since the critics had given me the green light with *Miss Mabel*.*

The 'New Movement' was that which had been heralded by the first performance in 1956 of *Look Back in Anger* by John Osborne (*b.*1929), and carried on by such playwrights as Harold Pinter (*b.*1930) and Arnold Wesker (*b.*1932). Beside plays by these playwrights and the drama of the Second World War by Willis Hall (*b.* 1929), *The Long and the Short and the Tall* (see p. 49), *Journey's End* speaks to and of a generation which has long passed. Yet it has survived as a play. Quite why this should be so, we shall be trying to analyse in these Notes.

Sherriff never married, and lived with his mother in his home in Esher and a farmhouse in Dorset until her death at an advanced age. He was a Fellow of the Society of Antiquaries and a Fellow of the Royal Society of Literature. He died in Kingston Hospital, Surrey, on 13 November 1975.

The original productions of *Journey's End*

The policy of the Stage Society, which operated from 1899 until the outbreak of the Second World War in 1939, was to produce for its members, once a month on a Sunday night when the theatres were not open to the public, a play of merit which would be unlikely to have a general appeal. Critics were invited to see a second performance in

No Leading Lady: an Autobiography, Gollancz, London, 1968, p. 351.

the afternoon of the Monday. In spite of the stage qualities which some people had already seen in *Journey's End*, the majority of the Society's committee were rather hostile to it, and no leading director would agree to take responsibility for producing it. As a last resort, the assignment was offered to a young theatrical all-round craftsman, James Whale. His enthusiasm and his skill as an imaginative scene designer had a lot to do with the eventual outcome. After many prominent actors, who were usually only too pleased to perform in Stage Society productions, had refused to play the main characters, the committee told Whale to appoint his own cast. He offered the leading role of Stanhope, the company commander, to a virtually unknown young actor. Lord Olivier (1907–89), as he later became, recorded his reaction:

> I took on all the opportunities I could grab . . . . Although I could recognise the possibilities of the part of Stanhope, I told James Whale, the director, I didn't think all that highly of the play.
> 'There's nothing but meals in it,' I complained.
> He replied: 'That's about all there was to think about in Flanders during the War.'*

He also revealed that he accepted the part 'as a sort of audition', since it was rumoured that the theatrical entrepreneur Basil Dean was looking for someone to play the title role in the stage version of P. C. Wren's *Beau Geste*, and would almost certainly be in the audience scouting for talent.

The first ever performance of *Journey's End* took place on Sunday 9 December 1928 on the stage of the Apollo Theatre, London. The applause of the sophisticated and critical audience was muted, but Mrs Sherriff cheered her son up afterwards by explaining, 'People don't clap when they're crying.'† The critics who saw the play the following day, however, were universally loud in their praise, and the doyen of them all, James Agate (1877–1947), devoted the whole of his weekly radio programme to it, ending with the ominous message:

> But you will never see this play. I have spoken with several managers, urging them to give you the opportunity of judging it for yourselves, but they are adamant in their belief that war plays have no audience in the theatre.‡

For a time it appeared that Agate was only too right. During the next fortnight the various managers remained adamant. War, they said,

---

*Laurence Olivier, *Confessions of an Actor*, Weidenfeld and Nicolson, London, 1982, pp. 50–1.
†This is confirmed by the mother of the author of these Notes, who was also in the audience that night.
‡Quoted in *No Leading Lady*, p. 64.

was an unpopular subject, and no war play had had even a moderate success. Besides, there was no woman in the cast. The apparent impasse was broken only on Christmas Eve, when Maurice Browne (1881–1955), an actor and minor producer, asked to see the script. Though he was a pacifist and conscientious objector, who had deliberately spent the war years in the U.S.A., or possibly *because* he was a pacifist, he was immediately impressed by the play's possibilities, and found the necessary backing from artistic friends to put it on the West End stage. The one condition that Sherriff made was that all the original cast should be offered the same roles as before, which meant that there was no part for Browne himself, who had set his heart on playing Osborne, the older second-in-command. All were available, and accepted eagerly, except Olivier, to whom the part of Beau Geste had duly been offered in the dressing-room immediately after his performance as Stanhope. He was philosophic about that particular episode in his career:

> Colin Clive as Stanhope rode triumphantly home for two years in *Journey's End*, which was brilliantly successful wherever it played . . . . That was the kind of dazzling whirligig a theatre success could sometimes achieve in the 1930s until about Munich time. That was what I had renounced.
>
> In the same period I went through seven flops, gaining not only experience but a happy collection of critical remarks and first-night approbation which constantly remarked, to my delight, upon my versatility.*

The first public performance of *Journey's End*, presented by Maurice Browne and produced again by James Whale, was at the Savoy Theatre on 21 January 1929. Whether it was the play itself or whether, as W. MacQueen Pope suggests, 'there is in the theatre a psychological moment when views as to subjects and manner of acting undergo a change, and that moment had come with regard to war plays, eleven years after the war was over',† or, as is more likely, there was a combination of causes, the critics and the audiences were unanimous in their approbation.

There remained the ultimate test, the production of the play on New York's Broadway, for which an entirely new cast was selected and shipped across the Atlantic in the liner *Aquitania*. Stanhope was played by Colin Keith Johnston, who had actually served in the war and won the Military Cross. The first-night audience revelled in the play; even the hard-bitten 'Butchers of Broadway', as the half-dozen leading dramatic critics were known, were ecstatic, and by noon of the

*Laurence Olivier, *Confessions of an Actor*, p. 51.
†W. MacQueen Pope, *The Footlights Flickered*, p. 225.

following day ticket touts were outside the theatre offering $5 tickets at $20 each.

Historical background to the play

The spark that ignited the conflagration that was the First World War was the assassination on 28 June 1914, at Sarajevo in Bosnia, of the heir to the Austrian throne. Austria declared war on neighbouring Serbia on 28 July. Russia mobilised her armies, whereupon Germany declared war not only on Russia but also, to safeguard her western front, on France, whom she invaded through Belgium. Britain had no alternative but to declare war on Germany, which she did on 4 August. The Germans advanced on their western front and got to within a few miles of Paris, but were driven back to the river Aisne by the Allied forces of Britain, the British Empire, and France. Both sides then settled down to the stalemate of trench warfare, which resulted in the bloody battles of the Somme, and elsewhere, and little gain to either side.

At the beginning of 1918, the German command prepared a massive offensive against the Allied line, and particularly that part defended by the British Third and Fifth Armies, which ran from the region of Arras to the river Oise in the south. St Quentin, opposite which was the section of the line held by the company in the play of *Journey's End*, lay some twenty miles north of the Oise. The British had fourteen divisions to defend the forty-mile sector of the line at whose centre was St Quentin. Against them, according to the official history of the campaign, the Germans massed forty-three combat divisions, backed by 2552 field batteries of artillery, 1636 heavy batteries, forty-eight super-heavy batteries, and 2306 trench mortars.*

As the play opens, the German assault is imminent.

Army ranks and organisation

Officer ranks in descending order of seniority – Field Marshal, General, Lieutenant-General, Major-General, Brigadier, Colonel, Lieutenant-Colonel, Major, Captain, Lieutenant, and Second Lieutenant.

The senior non-commissioned rank is that of Regimental Sergeant Major, followed by Sergeant-Major (of a company), Sergeant, Corporal, and Lance-Corporal.

A military force can have the following sub-divisions – army, corps, division, brigade (usually commanded by a Major-General or

Military Operations: France and Belgium, 1918, compiled by Brigadier-General Sir James E. Edmonds, Macmillan, London, 1935, pp. 152–3.

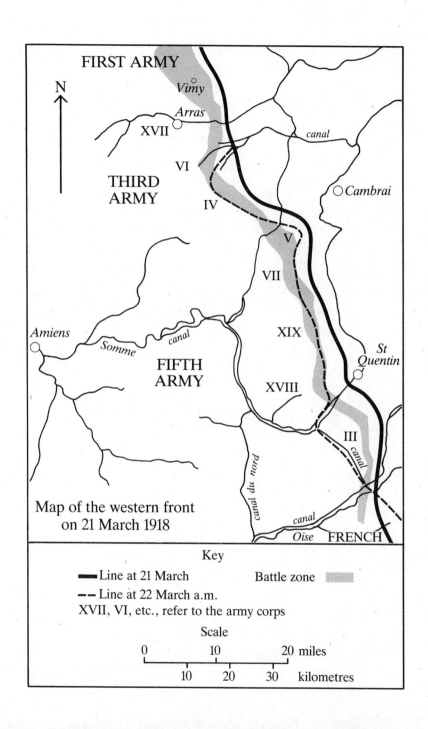

FIRST ARMY

N

Vimy

Arras

XVII

VI

THIRD
ARMY

IV

V

canal

○*Cambrai*

VII

XIX

Amiens

Somme *canal*

FIFTH
ARMY

XVIII

*St
Quentin*

III

canal

canal du nord

Map of the western front
on 21 March 1918

canal

Oise FRENCH

Key

▬▬Line at 21 March   Battle zone ▨

‒‒ Line at 22 March a.m.
XVII, VI, etc., refer to the army corps

Scale

0   10   20 miles

10   20   30   kilometres

Brigadier), regiment (Colonel), battalion (Lieutenant-Colonel), company (Captain), platoon, and section.

A note on the text

The original text of the play of *Journey's End* was published by Gollancz, London, in 1929. Editions in print at the time these Notes went to press were published by the following – Samuel French (Acting Edition), London, 1931; Heinemann Educational Books (edited by E. R. Wood in Hereford Plays), London, 1958; Penguin Books, London, new edition 1983. Two sets of page references are given in these Notes: the first is to the Penguin edition; the second is to the Heinemann Educational Books edition.

Part 2

Summaries
of JOURNEY'S END

The principal characters

The principal characters in the play of *Journey's End*, and the ones on whom the action centres, are the five officers of C Company, which as the play opens is taking up its position in the British front line at a time when the German assault upon it is imminent. Each is representative of a particular type of person. In order of appearance.

Lieutenant Osborne

About forty-five (p. 9/1). Second in command of the Company (p. 17/10). A schoolmaster (p. 41/38). Quiet, but firm and dependable. Known to his fellow officers as 'Uncle' (p. 17/10).

Second Lieutenant (Jimmy) Raleigh

About eighteen and just out from England (p. 16/9–10). Immature through lack of experience, and starry-eyed about the glory of war and about his schoolboy hero, Stanhope.

Captain (Dennis) Stanhope

Twenty-one (p. 13/6). Company commander. Even at his age a veteran of the trenches, and a holder of the Military Cross (p. 18/12). An excellent leader whose equilibrium has been shattered by his experiences.

Second Lieutenant Trotter

Middle-aged (p. 22/17). Presented, as a complete contrast to his fellow officers, as a figure of fun largely by reason of his lower middle-class origins, which are denoted by his habit of dropping aitches from his speech. His intuition and his courage, however, are never in doubt.

Second Lieutenant Hibbert

Early twenties (p. 28/24). A weakling whose collapse into an open display of cowardice is prevented by Stanhope's actions and persuasion.

A general summary

The action of the play takes place during the historical period from the evening of Monday 18 March, until dawn on Thursday 21 March 1918. The setting throughout is the minutely described underground dwelling place and office of the officers of C Company, dug out of the earth and connected by a flight of steps with the trench which is just behind the British front line. As Act I opens, preparations are being made for C Company to take its turn of duty at the front, and by its end we have been introduced to the principal characters. The former connection between Stanhope and Raleigh has been established and provides a source of conflict. Conditions in the trenches are illustrated, mainly through the dialogue.

In Act II, Scene 1 the wider theme of trench warfare is developed, and what Stanhope has seen as a conflict between himself and Raleigh comes to a head. Act II, Scene 2 is the most crucial scene in the play. In a conversation between Stanhope and his Sergeant-Major, the Company's predicament is emphasised, and the timing of the expected German assault and the Company's duty in opposing it are revealed. When the assault is launched, C Company is to delay the German advance but not to retreat under any circumstances. Further orders are brought by the Colonel. A party of men from the Company is to make a surprise raid on the German trenches in daylight and bring back a prisoner, who will then be interrogated about the composition of the forces in the German front line. Osborne and Raleigh are chosen to lead it. A confrontation between Stanhope and an hysterical Hibbert results in the latter abandoning his determination to report sick.

During Act III, Scene 1 the raid takes place. It is successful in that a prisoner is taken and information obtained, but Osborne is killed. In Act III, Scene 2 Stanhope, Trotter, and Hibbert go through with the planned party to celebrate the raid's completion. Raleigh cannot face joining them, and is reprimanded by Stanhope. As Act III, Scene 3 opens, the German bombardment, as a prelude to the assault, is about to begin. When it does, Raleigh is one of the first casualties. He is carried down into the dugout, where Stanhope tends to him in the few minutes before he dies. Then he himself goes out into the chaos and conflagration.

Detailed summaries

Act 1

Captain Hardy, commander of the Company which is being relieved by C Company, hands over in a somewhat jocular and casual manner to Osborne, whose insistence on the formalities being observed establishes his dependability. During their conversation, two sides of Stanhope emerge – the youth turned hard drinker by the effect on his nerves of continuous action; and the incomparable leader of men in battle conditions. Raleigh, newly posted to the Company from England, is brought in. He reveals in conversation with Osborne that he had wanted to join the same regiment as Stanhope because they had been at school together and because Stanhope is unofficially engaged to his sister. Now, he finds himself in the very Company commanded by his hero. Osborne gently stresses that Raleigh may find Stanhope rather changed. Stanhope and Trotter enter, and Stanhope calls for a bottle of whisky before even noticing Raleigh, and is then taken aback by his presence. At the end of supper, Trotter and Raleigh go on watch, relieving Hibbert, who disappears into one of the tunnels without eating. Stanhope reveals to Osborne his fears that Raleigh will tell his sister about the changes in his personality and his drinking habits. He is even prepared to censor Raleigh's letters. Osborne calms him down but has to help him to bed.

NOTES AND GLOSSARY:
Pages 9–13 (1–6)

close-cropped:	cut very short
as hard as nails:	tough
pack:	knapsack in which a soldier on active service carries his belongings
Cheero:	usually 'cheerio' = goodbye. Here, a drinking salute, today rendered as 'cheers'
line:	defensive position
rifle grenades:	anti-personnel bombs propelled by a rifle
Minnies:	(*slang*) mine-throwers, trench mortars (*German*: Minenwerfer). See p. 55 of these Notes for a fuller description by Ian Hay
bang-in:	exactly on target
Boche:	(*slang*) German
pavé:	(*French*) paving stones, cobbles
Lewis gun:	light machine gun, named after its American army inventor, Colonel Isaac Newton Lewis (1859–1931)
sap:	branch leading off a trench towards the opposing front line
transport lines:	depot from which men and supplies are taken to their destinations in the front line
funny:	peculiar, strange
trench stores:	ammunition and other equipment kept in the trenches

Jerry: (*slang*) German

Mills bombs: hand grenades, named after their manufacturer, Sir William Mills (1856–1932)

gum boots: waterproof rubber boots

dear young boy: the term is used here ironically

Drinking like a fish: drinking alcohol heavily

chap: fellow

put away: consume, drink

Valennes: town or village behind the lines

bear-baiting . . . cock-fighting: medieval spectator sports symbolising degeneracy and cruelty

leave: vacation from duty

jolly good fellow: traditional term of approval

all to blazes: shattered, dispersed

came to: regained his senses

hush it up: keep it a secret

Pages 14–18 (6–12)

sticks out a mile: is perfectly obvious

blithering: talking nonsense

log-book: official record

gas satchel: gas-mask container

bloody well: strong language used for emphasis

tip: piece of advice, especially with regard to horse racing

go like hell: move extremely quickly

lay supper: arrange the table for supper

you've got me: you have asked me a question I cannot answer

ration: standard restricted portion

Righto: (*upper-class colloquialism*) I agree

Boulogne: French port adjacent to the English coast

Rugby: Rugby School, a famous English public school

looking after the relief: supervising the handing over to his Company of that portion of the line

skipper of rugger: captain of rugby football

Barford: the name of a fictitious public school

kept wicket for the eleven: was wicket-keeper for the school cricket team

jolly good bat: excellent batsman (at cricket)

in the same class: of the same standard

colours: school award for sporting distinction

I bet: I am sure

MC: Military Cross, lowest of three grades of medal awarded to army officers for gallantry

big fluke: extraordinary piece of luck

base: army headquarters
detail: assign
bit my head off: reprimanded me
Pages 19–23 (13–17)
officially engaged: formally betrothed
tells on: affects
a dozen each with a cricket stump: at this time and until well after the Second World War, the most senior boys at many public schools were entitled to inflict corporal punishment
stand-to: state of general readiness for action
support line: defensive line which backs up the troops on duty at the front line proper
Bisley: famous British competition rifle-range
Wipers: (*slang*) Ypres
over the top: up out of the trenches and straight across the ground
Lancer: cavalry man
Very lights: signal flares, named after their inventor, the American Edward Very (1847–1910)
No Man's Land: space between the two opposing front lines
given you a turn: made you feel uneasy
chunks: roughly cut pieces
a leopard can't change its spots: proverbial expression meaning that a person's nature cannot change
stars of rank: a Captain carries a line of three stars on each shoulder
blasted: meaningless swear-word used for emphasis
Pages 24–8 (18–24)
pince-nez: (*French*) pair of spectacles without side pieces which clips on to the bridge of the nose
mess: place where servicemen eat
screw: portion in a twisted cone of paper
bloomin':   meaningless word which is used for emphasis and which usually denotes a speaker of the lower classes
'Ock der Kaiser': (*colloquial German* = Hoch der Kaiser) 'Up with the Kaiser!' The Kaiser was Wilhelm II, Emperor of Germany
turn in: go to bed
duty roll: rota of duty officers and men
dooty: mispronunciation of 'duty'
Aye, aye, sir: properly the Naval response to an order from a superior officer; here used jocularly

field of fire:	arc which a gun can cover
blinkin':	meaningless word used for emphasis
'ere:	here (used as an intrusive and meaningless epithet)
sniping:	aimed rifle fire from behind cover
neuralgia:	nerve pain

Pages 29–35 (25–35)

funk:	fright
done his bit:	performed his duty
awfully:	very
old man:	used as an affectionate term of respect
rot:	nonsense
kid:	boy
His people:	his parents
jolly:	very
Vimy Ridge:	key point in the battles around Arras in northern France. It was finally recaptured by a force of Canadian and Scottish troops in 1917, in a battle during which over 11,000 lives were lost
slimy:	disgusting
long live:	here used as an ironical toast
prig:	narrow-minded moralist
go west:	be destroyed
cheek:	impertinence
wanner:	want to, the contraction resulting from his speech being slurred because of drink
dustpan and brush . . . apron . . . lace:	references to the activities and costume of a house-maid

---

Act II, Scene 1

After the now predictable debate about food – this time it is the breakfast – and comparisons between life at home and at the front, Raleigh goes off to write a letter. Stanhope and Osborne discuss the implications of the news that the German assault is expected in two days' time and of the orders that the Company has received to combat it. Raleigh, on his way now to inspect the men's rifles, asks where to leave his letter for collection. He is surprised and embarrassed when Stanhope insists that he leaves it open. He tries to take it back, but Stanhope wrests it from him and orders him to carry on with his duty, even rounding on Osborne, who has tried to remonstrate with him. Ashamed, Stanhope then realises that he cannot bring himself to read the letter. Osborne offers to do it for him, and reads the relevant passage aloud. It is quite harmless, and very complimentary to Stanhope . . .

NOTES AND GLOSSARY:
Pages 36–40 (32–7)

rasher:	slice of bacon
gravy:	Mason is making fun of Trotter
familiar:	free in his speech
Lux:	brand of soap flakes
prize:	here used sarcastically
dumplings:	suet balls, a traditional accompaniment to boiled beef
Didn't 'arf:	'did not half', a lower-class rendering of a term of emphasis
bet your boots:	(*slang*) be absolutely sure
plate:	device in the mouth to which false teeth are attached
wiring parties:	sections of men detailed off to see to the repair or laying down of barbed wire barriers
braced up:	strengthened
me slippers . . . me pipe:	my slippers . . . my pipe
red, white and blue:	also the colours of the British national flag
'olly'ocks:	hollyhocks
'ite:	height
salient:	outward projecting line of defences
pear-drops:	a kind of sweet with a pervading taste
poops:	(*slang*) idiots
whizz-bangs:	onomatopoeic name applied colloquially by British troops to a particular kind of German shell in use from 1915 to 1918
down the line:	away from the front line
billets:	sleeping quarters
rugger field:	marked out area within which is the field of play in rugby football

Pages 41–5 (37–43)

reffing:	acting as referee
Harlequins:	famous English rugby football club
simply topping:	(*contemporary slang*) absolutely marvellous
Where did you play:	what position on the field did you play?
Wing three:	wing three-quarter, an attacking position for which speed is an asset
Tuppence:	two pennies (old currency). Osborne is jokingly suggesting that Raleigh should now have to pay to talk to someone of his eminence in sport
breeze it about:	tell people about it
jolly bucked:	very much elated
wind up:	nervous

genuine sort of chap: sincere kind of person
quartermaster-sergeant: non-commissioned officer in charge of supplies
front row of the stalls: traditionally the best seats in a theatre
nice plate of sardines: another example of Mason's 'familiarity'. It is the last dish likely to appeal to a man who has been drinking heavily
stick it: hold out
croquet: sport traditionally associated with garden lawns
potty: (*slang*) insane
You could have heard a pin drop: proverbial phrase indicating utter silence
pouches: pockets attached to a webbing belt
Pages 46–9 (44–8)
show: theatrical performance
Hippodrome: London variety theatre
George Robey: (1869–1954), English comedian
magazines: compartments attached to automatic rifles in which ammunition is stored
stick it down: moisten and close the flap of the envelope

Act II, Scene 2

Stanhope explains to the Company's Sergeant-Major, the senior non-commissioned officer, how he proposes to carry out the orders he has been given for when the German assault comes. It is quite clear to both of them what the fate of C Company will be. The Company's responsibilities are increased by further orders which the Colonel brings. A prisoner is to be seized from the German trenches in daylight. Osborne is to command this raid. The Colonel suggests that Raleigh should make the actual snatch of the prisoner. Stanhope at first demurs, but when the Colonel proposes selecting instead an officer from another company, he quickly and firmly agrees that Raleigh shall go. After the Colonel has left, Hibbert enters from his sleeping tunnel and announces that he is going to report sick. Stanhope refuses to let him do so and Hibbert strikes him. Stanhope threatens to shoot him if he tries to leave the dugout. Hibbert capitulates, whereupon Stanhope, by sheer force of personality and by appealing to Hibbert's feelings of duty and comradeship, calms him down and gets his support. Stanhope explains now to Osborne about the raid, which will take place the following afternoon. Osborne chooses the non-commissioned officer he would like to have to accompany him. The nine others in the party will be volunteers. Osborne and Trotter discuss the raid. To boost Hibbert's confidence, Stanhope accompanies him on his turn of duty, relieving Raleigh, who comes down into the dugout clearly elated at the prospect of the raid and at being chosen to participate in it.

NOTES AND GLOSSARY:
Pages 50–4 (48–54)

Have a whisky?: it is a sign both of Stanhope's rapport with his men and of the seriousness of the situation that he can offer a drink to a non-commissioned officer while giving him orders, and not forgo any respect

tot: measure, portion

look here: pay attention

down both flanks: the effect of this tactic, laying barbed wire barriers on each side of C Company's position between the front line and the support line, will be to offer some protection from lateral attack if (or, according to Stanhope's prediction, when) the companies on either side are beaten back from the front line

falling back: the Sergeant-Major is using a euphemism for 'retreat'

get through the gaps: that is, advance to take over the ground on either side of C Company which has been vacated by A and B Companies

Then we advance and win the war: ironical. The Sergeant-Major's response echoes the tone of the statement

Hoy!: ejaculatory statement

A surprise daylight raid . . .: the enemy will hardly expect a raid on their lines to be made in daylight, and some kind of natural light will help the raiding party to see where their target is. A screen of smoke from the British line will help to hide them from the enemy at the outset of their dangerous assignment

blow a hole . . . cut a hole: in this way, neither the British nor the German barbed wire defences will hinder the progress of the raiding party

collar: capture

guts: (*colloquial*) courage

so long: goodbye

rail-head: the farthest point of a railway

Whiting: a sea-fish, not considered much of a delicacy, but under active war conditions fresh fish would be a rarity

like hell: very badly

Pages 55–9 (54–9)

go down: also has the meaning of 'fall ill'

down the line: back to the base camp

my stuff: my belongings

shot for deserting: the standard punishment for deserting one's duty was to be shot

shirker: one who avoids his duty, but here also in the sense of 'malingerer', one who pretends to be ill to get off work

Striking a superior officer!: one of the most serious crimes in the armed services

blasted funk: unutterable coward

fighting chance: luck made more attainable by making a supreme effort

Not till dinner-time: the joking implication is that at dinner Mason will serve up the same concoction and call it onion soup

onion tea: Stanhope is responding to one joke with another

Pages 60–4 (59–65)

toch-emmas: (*army slang*) trench-mortars

volunteers: it is a sign of an excellently led company that its commanding officer can ask for volunteers from among the men for an especially hazardous mission and expect to get them

frowsy: stuffy

'Tell me, mother . . .': from *Ruthless Rhymes for Heartless Homes* (1899) by Harry Graham (1874–1936)*

tied bits o' red rag: the implication is that the Germans realised the purpose of the tactic, and showed that they were prepared for the subsequent operation

cropping up: coming to the surface, materialising. The reference is to the way the taste of onions tends to recur while they are in the digestive system

***Alice's Adventures in Wonderland*:** the classic English fantasy by Lewis Carroll – Charles Lutwidge Dodgson (1832–98), a mathematical lecturer at Oxford University. It was published in 1865

'How doth the little crocodile . . .': these verses are in Chapter 2, and are in part a parody of a verse by Isaac Watts (1674–1748), theologian and poet, in *Divine Songs for Children* (1715), 'How doth the little busy bee . . .'. There is a deliberate contrast intended between the sophisticated wit of Carroll and the

*I am indebted to Stewart Sanderson for this reference.

	down-to-earth humour of Graham, quoted by Trotter
on the go:	active
hay-fever:	condition, aggravated by pollen, which affects the nose and throat
my old lady:	my wife
I say!:	expression of wonder

Act III, Scene 1

As the deadline approaches, Stanhope expresses to the Colonel his doubts about the timing and the organisation of the preliminaries to the raid on the German lines. The Colonel is adamant that it must go ahead as planned. Osborne and Raleigh are left alone to while away the minutes before they have to go. Stage directions and sound effects indicate that the raid is taking place. The Sergeant-Major and two armed soldiers bring a prisoner down into the dugout. It is only after the Colonel has interrogated the young German and expressed his satisfaction at the success of the raid that he remembers to ask Stanhope how the raiding party has fared. Stanhope reveals obliquely that Osborne and six of the ten men have been killed. Raleigh comes down the steps in a state of shock. The Colonel enthuses over him, and leaves. Together, Stanhope and Raleigh suffer their reaction to and grief at the loss of Osborne.

NOTES AND GLOSSARY:
Pages 65–70 (66–73)

arrange the placing of reserves:	the inference is that the precise stationing of troops to support those in the front line will depend on what particular German regiments are directly opposing them
because of dinner:	a touch of sarcasm
bombs:	that is, smoke bombs
red rags:	see note to pages 60–4 (59–65)
rum:	an alcoholic drink distilled from sugar-cane or molasses. It was issued to men in action, an extra tot being given as a morale booster in exceptional circumstances, as is the case here
If you think they would:	the Colonel's general attitude, uncertainty, bluffness and, later, tactlessness, reflect the accusations of incompetence levelled at the time and later at the British high command in France
like blazes:	(*slang*) furiously
bundle:	hustle unceremoniously

handy: convenient, to hand

papers and things: anything which might give information to the enemy in the case of their owner being killed or captured

tuck me up in bed: see Act I, page 34 (31)

muzzy: dazed

parapet: here, a raised bank of earth protecting soldiers in the trench from the fire of the enemy in front of them

'"The time has come", the Walrus said . . .': another piece of nonsense verse by Lewis Carroll, from Chapter 4 of *Through the Looking-Glass and What Alice Found There* (1872), the sequel to *Alice's Adventures in Wonderland*. Osborne is trying to take Raleigh's mind off the impending raid

'And why the sea is boiling hot . . .': Raleigh knows, and quotes, the following two lines

Now we're off: Osborne is quick to capitalise on any possibility of a new subject of conversation

New Forest: once an ancient royal hunting ground; it is a large area of forest land situated in the county of Hampshire

Lyndhurst: town in the New Forest

Pages 71–7 (73–80)

William the Conqueror: William I (1027–87), the first Norman king of England

Sussex: English county adjoining Hampshire

Stane Street: the road started from Chichester

Bignor Hill: at Bignor are the remains of a Roman villa which had particular significance in the third and fourth centuries AD. Interestingly enough, the archaeological site which Sherriff acquired several years after writing *Journey's End* (see p. 9) is only a few miles to the south-east of Bignor

lays it carefully on the table: a pipe-smoker normally knocks out the burning ash of the tobacco when he has finished. The stage direction, implying that he leaves his pipe still alight, intending to return to it, is an example of dramatic irony

put up a good show: put on a good performance

sonny: kindly term of address to a boy

in somewhat poor German: the author has to sustain the audience's suspension of disbelief in the action while enabling those who do not know any German to follow the dialogue, which he does by employing a mixture of poor German and broken English

Gestern abend: yesterday evening

a feather in our cap: a distinction for us. The phrase comes from an ancient custom among Asian and north American tribes of adding a feather to their headdress for each enemy killed

awfully nice: this ironic observation, and its repetition ten lines below, is the nearest Stanhope gets during the play to a display of anger against authority

---

Act III, Scene 2

The contrast between the opening situation in this scene and the close of the last has a deliberate dramatic intensity. The celebration dinner is going ahead, without Osborne. Raleigh is missing, too. Stanhope is in the middle of an indelicate story. The hilarity and the laughter are forced, and sustained only by liberal quantities of drink. It is therefore hardly surprising that the party ends in wrangling and an altercation between Stanhope and Hibbert. It appears that Raleigh should have been with them earlier, and when he does come into the dugout, he refuses his dinner, explaining that he has had something to eat with the men. Stanhope reprimands him for taking the men's rations and for insulting his fellow officers by not joining them. When Raleigh still refuses to eat, on the grounds that he cannot do so for thinking of Osborne, Stanhope responds by pointing out that in Osborne he has lost 'The one man I could trust – my best friend . . .'. Raleigh realises that he has made a misjudgment, but Stanhope, at breaking point now, and with no Osborne to calm him, cannot accept his apology.

NOTES AND GLOSSARY:
Pages 77–9 (80–3)

mam'sel: (*French*) mademoiselle = miss

have it your own way: a sexual pun is intended

scream: hilarious fellow

tarts: prostitutes

'E's orf again: He's off again, that is, he's started again

bubbly: champagne

joy-ride: pleasure trip

Maidenhead: town in the county of Berkshire, about thirty miles from the centre of London

sixty: sixty miles per hour

Skindles: name of a night-club

chuck: throw

hair on end:	terrified
Shanks' mare:	to ride Shanks' mare is to walk, the shank being that part of the leg from the knee to the foot
Bethune:	town in northern France, behind the British lines
Margate Pier:	Margate is a well-known English seaside resort

Pages 80–6 (84–91)

say when!:	tell me when to stop pouring
Wo!:	whoa, interjection often associated with persuading a horse to stop
decent spot:	in this context, a large measure
I'm game!:	I'm willing
blabbing:	talking too much
fresh as a daisy:	feeling invigorated
bloke:	fellow
sucking up:	(*slang*) ingratiating oneself

Act III, Scene 3

Mason, the cook, wakes the officers, who prepare to join their men in the trenches as the German bombardment that will herald the assault becomes imminent. The shells start to fall on the Company's position. Trotter and Raleigh leave the dugout, while Stanhope stays to receive any messages and to write up his notes. He calls for Hibbert, who has not yet appeared. The cry of 'Stretcher bear-ers!' indicates that the Company has suffered its first casualty of the morning. Hibbert is reluctant to move, making every excuse to delay, but Mason cleverly and diplomatically asks to join him. They go out together. The shelling intensifies. The Sergeant-Major reports to Stanhope that Raleigh is badly injured, and is ordered to bring him down into the dugout. Stanhope insists that a stretcher is found to take the injured officer back to the base, but Raleigh dies before it can be brought. Stanhope, deeply affected by his death, goes up the steps. Seconds later, the dugout disintegrates under the weight of shell-fire.

NOTES AND GLOSSARY:
Pages 86–95 (92–103)

lathering:	soaping, as a prelude to shaving
Wash and brush-up:	standard announcement of additional facilities available in a men's public toilet for washing and generally tidying oneself
buck up:	(*colloquial*) be quick
sambridges:	humorous pronunciation of 'sandwiches'
with gusto:	enthusiastically
Runner:	messenger

'There's a long, long trail a-winding': popular nostalgic song of the time. Stanhope's response is to pretend to be rewarding a busker. Trotter's reply is in kind

right down to the support line: see note to Act II, Scene 2, pages 50–4 (48–54)

About 'arf again: that is, about fifty per cent more than the usual allowance

bully beef: canned beef

pâté de foie gras: the ultimate delicacy, made from goose liver. Stanhope is being ironical, but Mason is still quite up to making a pertinent and amusing retort

Fosse Way: name of a Roman road in England, but here attributed to a trench

a Blighty one: a wound which is serious enough to necessitate the sufferer being returned to England

Part 3

Commentary

Realism in *Journey's End*

Two questions may be asked about a drama whose setting and situations claim to be realistic. How much is true to life? And how much is true?

Sherriff himself wrote:

> A lot of fun was made out of the experienced West End managers who had refused the play and thrown away a fortune, but it was the easy old game of being wise after the event. They had done their best to get war plays across to the public, and all without exception had failed. The only thing they hadn't taken account of was that *Journey's End* happened to be the first war play that kept its feet in the Flanders mud. All the previous plays had aimed at higher things: they carried 'messages', 'sermons against war', symbolic revelations. The public knew enough about war to take all that for granted. What they had never been shown before on the stage was how men really lived in the trenches, how they talked and how they behaved.*

There were other pointers to the public's attitude. A poet, Edmund Blunden (1896–1974), had with *Undertones of War* (1928) just published an autobiography which covered his life as an army officer in France during the war. Two others, Robert Graves (1895–1985) with *Good-Bye to All That* (1929) and Siegfried Sassoon (1886–1967) with *Memoirs of an Infantry Officer* (1930), were shortly to do so. The time gap between the end of the war in 1918 and the publication of the first of these accounts ten years later had allowed their authors to distil their experiences into the raw material of distinguished prose and the public to come to the realisation that there were after all things which needed to be recorded for posterity. So John Keegan could say in 1976:

> Blunden's, Graves's and Sassoon's [accounts] have not only stood up well to the passage of time; everything about them suggests that they will continue to be read, not as background material for an understanding of the Great War, or as documentary evidence, but as moving and enduring expressions of truth about how man confronts the inevitability of death.†

No Leading Lady, p. 109.
†*The Face of Battle*, p. 288.

If we look closer at these factual prose records, we can find passages that reflect or even echo the experiences which Sherriff's characters undergo in *Journey's End*. Edmund Blunden spent a month in the trenches only ten miles to the north of St Quentin early in 1918, being returned for duty in England just a day or so before the German assault on 21 March. He records the silence to which Raleigh refers in Act I (p. 20/14), and describes the desolation of the scene.

> Our position was extensive, and included two 'strong points', called Quentin Redoubt and Gauche Wood. The actual front trench east of these was a straggling ill-sited concern. West of them stretched a valley and a railway, parallel with the front, and a ridge, again parallel; under the ridge, in a cutting, battalion headquarters and supporting companies lived; thence, overland, one walked by the duckboards or the tramway back to a group of buildings commanding the support battalion's positions, called Revelon. The grassy table-land was incised with trenches, some achieved, more inchoate – too many intentions of trenches, perhaps. A little wire made the 'system' slightly stronger. This area was all to be involved in the battle of March 21, of which some rumours were already adrift among us, and the battalion was used not only to hold the position but also, simultaneously, to fortify it in every detail.*

While the particular experiences Robert Graves describes took place in 1915 farther to the north on the Cambrin–Cuinchy section of the line, even within a single page of his account we find that Stanhope's need for drink is no exaggeration, and that the action of the humane German officer recalled by Osborne in Act II, Scene 1 (p. 42/39) is no isolated piece of fiction:

> From the morning of September 24th to the night of October 3rd I had in all eight hours of sleep. I kept myself awake and alive by drinking about a bottle of whisky a day. I had never drank it before and have seldom drunk it since; it certainly was good then. We had no blankets, greatcoats, or waterproof sheets. We had not time or material to build new shelters, and the rain continued . . . . On the morning of the 27th a cry was heard from No Man's Land. It was a wounded man of the Middlesex [Regiment] who had recovered consciousness after two days. He was close to the German wire. Our men heard it and looked at each other. We had a lance-corporal called Baxter and he was tender-hearted. He was the man to boil up a special dixie of tea for the sentries of his section when they came off duty. When he heard the wounded man cry out he ran up and down the trench calling for a volunteer to come out with him and bring the

---

Undertones of War, Cobden-Sanderson, London, 1928, p. 266.

man in. Of course no one would go; it was death to put one's head over the trench. He came running to ask me. I excused myself as the only officer in the company. I said I would come out with him at dusk, but I would not go now. So he went out himself. He jumped quickly over the parapet, then strolled across waving a handkerchief; the Germans fired at him to frighten him, but he came on, so they let him come up close. They must have heard the Middlesex man themselves. Baxter continued towards them and, when he got up to the Middlesex man, he stopped and pointed to show the Germans what he was at. Then he dressed the man's wounds, gave him a drink of rum and some biscuit that he had with him, and told him he would be back again for him in the evening. He did come back for him with a stretcher-party and the man eventually recovered.[*]

Of the setting for his play, Sherriff wrote:

A Company Headquarters dugout in the front line made a perfect natural setting for the theatre. It was usually one of a chain of dugouts linked together by short tunnels, each with its own way up to the trench by a steep flight of steps. The tunnel to one side would lead to the dugout where some of the officers slept, the opposite one to the quarters of the signallers and runners, and the place where the cook-batman prepared the meals. This made it easy to move the characters in and out as needed. An officer would go up the steps to take his turn of duty in the trenches: the one he relieved would come in for a meal, then go off stage to the adjoining dugout for some sleep when he was no longer required. With a little simple planning you could bring the characters together and disperse them easily, and I had lived in those murky underground caverns for so many months that I knew them as intimately as the room I was then working in.[†]

Thereby, whether by intention or subconsciously, he was observing with the greatest of effect the eighteenth-century French interpretation of one of the classic unities of drama supposed to have been prescribed by Aristotle (384–322BC), that the whole action of a tragedy should be in a single place.

The official history of the war records that late in the afternoon of 20 March 1918 some raids were made on the German lines and a few prisoners taken (as happens in Act III, Scene 1), and that during the night ground fog developed (as Trotter observes in Act III, Scene 2, p. 83/88).[‡] The German bombardment opened at about 5a.m. At

[*]*Good-Bye to All That: an Autobiography*, Cape, London, 1929, pp. 211–12.
[†]*No Leading Lady*, pp. 35–6.
[‡]*Military Operations: France and Belgium, 1918*, p. 161.

9.40a.m. the German infantry overran the XVIII Corps which was defending that part of the line opposite St Quentin, and only fifty men of the eight battalions which it comprised managed to fight their way back to the battle zone behind the original British line.

We have two eye-witness, or rather ear-witness, accounts, one from the German and one from the British side, of the ferocity of the bombardment with which the play of *Journey's End* closes. Leutnant Herbert Sulzbach was in charge of a battery of Field Artillery actually in St Quentin.

> There were thousands of batteries besides our own firing. The noise was so deafening that I could only order the fire by using a whistle, but the spirit and enthusiasm of the gunners was so tremendous that I hardly needed to give them orders, they just kept on slamming shell after shell into the breech.*

Private Jim Brady was with the 43rd Field Ambulance, Royal Army Medical Corps:

> We were deployed at advance posts facing St Quentin and awoke to the thunder of a thousand guns and the shattering blast of shells. We were in a dugout, thirty feet deep, but even so we were absolutely scared stiff. Cracks were appearing in the rafters and sand was running down on us from sandbags that had burst. The gas-curtain half-way down the stairway had been torn to shreds, and we could feel the blast sweeping in with every shell burst.†

By 29 March the Germans had pushed back the British front line opposite St Quentin a distance of thirty miles. But there, or thereabouts, it held, while the German morale all along the line was faltering. It was the beginning of the end of the war.

Yet in the final analysis, however realistic the historical background, the basic situation, and the setting, *Journey's End* is still a play, the aim of whose author was to entertain while holding up a mirror to life. It is not a documentary, in that its characters are wholly fictional. Sometimes a blend of the two forms, the fictional play and the documentary drama, can cause confusion, as it did in Britain in 1988 in the case of the BBC television play, *Tumbledown* by Charles Wood, based on the successful British military campaign in 1982 to recapture the Falkland Islands from its Argentinian invaders. Instead of making all the characters entirely imaginary, however, Wood (and the BBC) chose to base the play on the experiences of a real character who was severely wounded in one of the battles and survived. The heart of the

*Quoted in Lyn Macdonald, *The Roses of No Man's Land*, new edition, Macmillan, London, 1984, p. 248.
†Quoted in *The Roses of No Man's Land*, p. 248.

considerable controversy which ensued was thus how much was truth, how much was invention, and how much a manipulation of the truth.

Language and dialogue

Sherriff described his technique thus:

> Dialogue came easily: I merely had to write down what people said. I didn't have to turn up the dictionary for flowery words and hunt through my book of synonyms. The other characters walked in without invitation. I had known them all so well in the trenches that the play was an open house for them.*

As we have seen (p. 15), the main characters in the play represent particular types of men with inherent characteristics, and two of them (Stanhope and Raleigh) originally belonged to an unfinished novel, the playing out of whose main theme of hero-worship was to have been spread over several years, but in the play takes only a few days. In creating the dialogue for his play, Sherriff may well have been, and probably was, to a certain extent playing over in his mind what he had heard men say in similar circumstances, but he was also attributing a particular form of speech to each type, and reflecting the language that playgoers of his time would expect to hear from that kind of person. In reading the play, we must bear in mind not just the person who is making a particular remark, but the kind of person he represents. Let us take two typical, but at first sight rather ordinary, passages of dialogue.

RALEIGH: Did you play rugger?
OSBORNE: Yes. But mostly reffing at school in the last few years.
RALEIGH: Are you a schoolmaster, then?
OSBORNE: Yes. I must apologise.
RALEIGH: Oh, I don't mind schoolmasters. (*Hastily*) I – I – mean, I never met one outside a school.
OSBORNE: They do get out sometimes.
RALEIGH (*laughing*): Who did you play for?
OSBORNE: The Harlequins.
RALEIGH: I say, really!
OSBORNE: I played for the English team on one great occasion.
RALEIGH: What! For *England*!
OSBORNE: I was awfully lucky to get the chance. It's a long time ago now.
RALEIGH (*with awe*): Oh, but, good Lord! that must have been simply topping. Where did you play?

*No Leading Lady, p. 35.

OSBORNE: Wing three.

RALEIGH: I say, I – I never realized – you'd played for England?

OSBORNE: Tuppence to talk to me now! Anyhow, don't breeze it about.

RALEIGH: Don't the others know?

OSBORNE: We never talk about rugger.

RALEIGH: They ought to know. It'd make them feel jolly bucked.

OSBORNE (*laughing*): It doesn't make much difference out here!

(Act II, Scene 1, pp. 40–1/37–8)

Here is the impressionable (as we know already from his hero-worship of Stanhope) youth, not long out of a sheltered existence in an all-male boarding school, to whom a schoolmaster is an object of awe and respect, suddenly discovering that this, to him, elderly man is not just friendly and prepared to give the time to talk to him, but also a very distinguished sportsman, in a field of activity in which the public schools excelled.

MASON: Your tea, sir!

STANHOPE: Keep it hot, Mason.

MASON: Will you take this cup, Mr Osborne?

STANHOPE: Take the other in to Mr Hibbert, in there.

MASON: Very good, sir. (*He goes into* HIBBERT'S *dugout.*)

STANHOPE: Shan't be long, Uncle. (*He goes up the steps.*)

OSBORNE: Righto.

    (MASON *returns*)

MASON: Will you have cut bread and butter – or shall I bring the loaf, sir?

OSBORNE: Cut it, Mason, please.

MASON: Just bringing the jam separately?

OSBORNE: Yes.

MASON: Very good, sir.

(Act II, Scene 2, pp. 60–1/61)

This little exchange, about the tea, the bread, the butter, and the jam, reminds us that while Stanhope is a man of action for whom duty is paramount and giving orders a natural concomitant, he is also sufficiently understanding of his men to think of Hibbert's predicament and immediate needs, and to be seen to be so. To Osborne, even under conditions in the trenches, the niceties and etiquette of normal middle-class life must be preserved – to be served with his bread sliced and buttered, rather than to have to cut it himself, to have the jam brought separately, even if it is in its pot rather than in a dish, and to say 'please' to a servant.

Theatre-goers of the 1920s and 1930s would be more likely to patronise than respect a sympathetic character from a working-class background. So Sherriff makes Trotter a rather ridiculous figure, with an accent to match. Trotter speaks no recognisable regional dialect of English. He is typified by his dropped aitches and occasional variations from received pronunciation, for example, 'dooty' for 'duty'. Mason, on the other hand, in speech as well as demeanour, is the epitome of the superior servant of the times, a type immortalised by P. G. Wodehouse (1881–1975) in his incomparable stories about Jeeves.

Heroism as a theme in *Journey's End*

'What [the public] had never been shown before on the stage was how men really lived in the trenches, how they talked and how they behaved.'* We have seen (above pp. 31–2) that *Journey's End* mirrors the way men lived under those circumstances and (above p. 10 and p. 34) offers a representation of how they talked and what they talked about. Many members of the public would have had a good idea of these things, too, either from their own experience or from talking to friends and relations who had survived or who had been on leave from the trenches. What was never talked about, either because it was too personal or too painful or simply too intangible, was how they behaved. This, in particular, gives to *Journey's End* its lasting interest and to the men who participated in the ghastly business a graphic, and fitting, memorial.

A turn of duty in the trenches involved manning the defences against whatever offensive the enemy could devise (lightning attacks, mortar bombs, grenades, shelling, and also gas, a hazard which is only implied, not experienced, in *Journey's End*), making hazardous sorties out into No Man's Land, sometimes even raiding the opposing trenches, and suffering the tension of waiting, as happens in the play, for a major assault against which there is no real defence and from which there is no retreat. All this was done under conditions of appalling deprivation and discomfort – as witness, the exchange:

OSBORNE: Where do the men sleep?
HARDY: *I* don't know. The sergeant-major sees to that.
(Act I, p. 11/3)

The heroism displayed by the characters in *Journey's End* takes various forms. Nowhere in the play is there mention of any cause for which they are fighting, nor is any hatred expressed against the enemy. On the contrary, as Raleigh remarks (Act II, Scene 1, p. 42/39), 'The Germans are really quite decent, aren't they? I mean outside the newspapers?' To which Osborne responds in the affirmative. The German boy taken prisoner is deliberately drawn as pathetic and

*No Leading Lady, p. 109.

bewildered, and is treated with kindness and consideration by the Sergeant-Major (Act III, Scene 1, pp. 74–5/77–8). Duty to King and country is the simple and obviously the sole motivation, and bravery is rewarded by medals. 'How topping if we both get the MC!', observes Raleigh (Act III, Scene 1, p. 70/72). That the ten ordinary soldiers who accompany them on their dangerous exploit are volunteers (Act II, Scene 2, p. 60/60) cannot be too highly emphasised, in the same way as the fact that only four of them return (Act III, Scene 2, p. 76/79). As Sherriff himself explained: '[The characters in the play] were simple, unquestioning men who fought the war because it seemed the only right and proper thing to do. Somebody had got to fight it, and they had accepted the misery and suffering without complaint.'*

There is a much deeper sense of heroism in Osborne, a man fully aware of the implications of what he is undertaking, as he chats away to Raleigh before the raid, trying to take his much younger companion's mind off what is before them, and thus avoiding any hint of what the fate of many of the party is likely to be. For all of them are aware that the Germans are expecting something of the kind (Act III, Scene 1, p. 67/68). To go calmly to an almost certain death is one thing: to sit around, waiting quietly for the moment to come calls for extra qualities of heroism.

A different kind of heroism is needed, in the light of Osborne's death, to go through with the dinner-party which had been planned as a celebration of the raid, and for the officers to force themselves into a mood of outward jollification. It is an attitude generated by the circumstances to which they have become hardened, though it is beyond the comprehension of Raleigh, who was so recently a mere schoolboy, but during the raid itself became a man.

In the last scene, as they prepare for the hopeless defence of the line, both Stanhope and Trotter can joke and gently tease each other, and there is even something heroic about the final exit of the despicable Hibbert, determined not to give way to his fear in the presence of the understanding cook-batman.

The conflicts in *Journey's End*

The basis of the conflict between nations and the differences in national temperament between those that fought on opposite sides of it, without which there would have been no *Journey's End*, are never mentioned in the play. There was, at the time it was written, no need to do so. The unquestioning nationalism which is inherent throughout *Journey's End* had been clearly expounded on the stage more than three hundred years earlier, in *Henry V* by William Shakespeare

*No Leading Lady, p. 72.

(1564–1616), and in particular in the King's speech before the battle of Agincourt, which ends:

> This story shall the good man teach his son;
> And Crispin Crispian shall ne'er go by,
> From this day to the ending of the world,
> But we in it shall be remembered;
> We few, we happy few, we band of brothers;
> For he to-day that sheds his blood with me
> Shall be my brother; be he ne'er so vile,
> This day shall gentle his condition;
> And gentlemen in England now a-bed
> Shall think themselves accursed they were not here,
> And hold their manhoods cheap whiles any speaks
> That fought with us upon Saint Crispin's day.
>
> (Act IV, Scene 3)

These are, too, very much the sentiments with which Stanhope tries to bolster the confidence of Hibbert in Act II, Scene 2 of *Journey's End*. And though today's readers may find this kind of expression of nationalism outmoded as well as outdated, it was still common currency during the Second World War, to the extent that the famous film of Shakespeare's *Henry V* (1944), with Laurence Olivier directing as well as playing the title role, was by Olivier's own account inspired by the Ministry of Information, which instructed him to make it as propaganda for the British war effort.*

In *Journey's End* conflicts in attitudes to duty and the way it is performed are inferred in the interchange between Captain Hardy and Osborne in Act I, which also serves to highlight the different, and opposing, views about Stanhope's ability to command. The inherent conflict, which has an historical foundation, between the officers actually in the front line and those who commanded from behind the lines, is implied in Stanhope's exchanges with the Colonel in Act II, Scene 2 (pp. 52–4/51–3) and in Act III, Scene 1 (p. 76/79). The main conflict in the play, however, is a personal one, between Stanhope and Raleigh.

J. C. Trewin, writing only twenty or so years after the first production of *Journey's End*, stated that 'one of the legitimate if minor objections' to the play which now had to be made was 'the piece of plot-contrivance by which young Raleigh is sent to Stanhope's company, to the hero he had worshipped at school'.† Now, the hero-worship of Dennis Stanhope by young Jimmy Raleigh was, as we have seen (p. 7), the theme of the unfinished novel whose basic element

---

*Confessions of an Actor, p. 97.
†J. C. Trewin, *Dramatists of Today*, Staples Press, London, 1953, p. 145.

Sherriff transplanted to his play about the western front, though there was no reason, until the publication of *No Leading Lady* in 1968, why anyone should have known that. But to Sherriff, and thus to any member of the audience or reader of *Journey's End*, without that element there would be no essence of personal conflict in the play, and indeed possibly no play. The basic situation to which J. C. Trewin raised an objection is not just legitimate, but essential. It is, too, far more of a natural circumstance in the context of the play than a mere 'piece of plot-contrivance'. For what is known colloquially as the 'old boy network', whereby social or political or business favours are more easily obtained from someone who was at the same public school as oneself, or merely at another of the leading public schools, operates even now, though to a lesser extent than it did at the time of the First World War. So does nepotism. What is more likely, then, than that a young man who asked his uncle to put him into the same battalion as his hero (and prospective brother-in-law), should, whatever General Raleigh said to him openly (Act I, p. 18/12), have ended up in the same company, under the guidance, as well as the command, of Stanhope?

It is this basic and perfectly probable situation, then, that leads to the personal conflict between Stanhope and Raleigh, and ultimately to Raleigh's death. The conflict surfaces through the business of Raleigh's letter at the end of Act I, and comes to a head in Act III, Scene 2, when Stanhope, having taken Raleigh to task for joining the men rather than his fellow-officers, loses his temper when Raleigh refuses to eat the dinner which has been left for him. Just before that happens, however, comes the following exchange (p. 85/90):

STANHOPE: What are you looking at?
RALEIGH (*lowering his head*): Nothing.
STANHOPE: Anything – *funny* about me?
RALEIGH: No. (*After a moment's silence*, RALEIGH *speaks in a low halting voice.*) I'm awfully sorry, Dennis, if – if I annoyed you by coming to your company.
STANHOPE: What on *earth* are you talking about? What do you mean?
RALEIGH: You resent my being here.
STANHOPE: Resent you *being* here?
RALEIGH: Ever since I came –
STANHOPE: I don't know what you mean. I resent you being a damn fool, that's all . . .

The fact of the matter is that Stanhope *does* resent Raleigh's presence in the company because of his continual fear that Raleigh will reveal to the family, and especially to Madge, how his nerves have been shattered and his character changed under the pressure of his experiences at the front. This resentment has surfaced earlier, too, as an inner conflict when at first he does not agree to Raleigh being sent on the raid (Act II, Scene 2, pp. 53–4/53). It is a different kind of resentment, however, in that he is put in the unfortunate position of feeling protective towards the boy.

The conflict between them is only intensified by Raleigh's inane apology for his failure to understand Stanhope's ability to submerge his feelings (Act III, Scene 2, p. 86/91), and is still operating the following morning when Stanhope, by not even raising his head from what he is writing, does not properly respond to Raleigh's question or to his gesture of farewell (Act III, Scene 3, p. 89/96). While Stanhope's apparent insensitivity to Osborne's death is itself a revelation of another inner conflict, between his devotion to his friend and confidant and his duty to his junior officers. Only at the end of the play is the conflict between himself and Raleigh resolved, but by then it is too late.

The clash between Stanhope and Hibbert in Act II, Scene 2 is a case of a strong will overpowering a faint one, for Hibbert's conflict is really within himself. His weakness in other directions is demonstrated by his preoccupation with pornographic postcards (Act III, Scene 2, pp. 78–9/82–3), and his subsequent crass foolishness in answering back to what is an order from his commanding officer (pp. 81–2/86).

The place of humour in *Journey's End*

According to Sherriff's own recollection, the broadcast by James Agate which followed the original production of *Journey's End* contained the words: 'Lest you think it is a sombre, unrelieved tragedy I must tell you of a cook-batman whose every appearance brought the house down . . .'.* The English have a propensity for making jokes under circumstances of utmost stress or danger, even if they are often not very good jokes – the piece of by-play between Stanhope and Trotter in Act III, Scene 3 (pp. 87–8/94) is a perfect example. Shakespeare was a master of the use of humour to relieve tragic tension while heightening in retrospect the horror of a situation, the most famous instance of this being the appearance of the drunken porter to answer the knocking on the gate in *Macbeth*, Act II, Scene 3, immediately after the murder of Duncan and before its discovery.

In the same way, Sherriff deliberately employs in *Journey's End*, in the form of Mason, the cook-batman, a character whose activities and actions evoke humorous responses which momentarily divert the audience's attention while the next link in the play's tragic development heads for its crisis point. The humour also enlivens what otherwise would be the least interesting events and passages of realism, the

*Quoted in *No Leading Lady*, p. 64.

appearance of and eternal conversations about meals. Nor is it one-sided:

OSBORNE: What kind of soup is this, Mason?
MASON: It's yellow soup, sir.
OSBORNE: It's got a very deep yellow flavour.

(Act I, p. 24/19)

And again:

MASON: Will you have a nice cup of tea, sir?
STANHOPE: Can you guarantee it's nice?
MASON: Well, sir – it's a bit oniony, but that's only because of the saucepan.
STANHOPE: In other words, it's onion soup with tea-leaves in it?
MASON: Not till dinner-time, sir.
STANHOPE: All right, Mason. Bring two cups of onion tea. One for Mr Hibbert.

(Act II, Scene 2, p. 59/59)

The best lines on the subject, however, are generally given to Mason.

TROTTER: What a lovely smell of bacon!
MASON: Yes, sir. I reckon there's enough smell of bacon in 'ere to last for dinner.
TROTTER: Well, there's nothing like a good fat bacon rasher when you're as empty as I am.
MASON: I'm glad you like it fat, sir.
TROTTER: Well, I like a bit o' lean, too.
MASON: There *was* a bit of lean in the middle of yours, sir, but it's kind of shrunk up in the cooking.
TROTTER: Bad cooking, that's all. Any porridge?
MASON: Oh, yes, sir. There's porridge.
TROTTER: Lumpy, I s'pose?
MASON: Yes, sir. Quite nice and lumpy.
TROTTER: Well, take the lumps out o' mine.
MASON: And just bring you the gravy, sir? Very good, sir.

(Act II, Scene 1, p. 36/32)

Though Stanhope and Osborne can seriously discuss Trotter's lack of imagination (Act II, Scene 1, p. 44/42) and in doing so display an extraordinary attitude of class-condescension, Trotter is not only a genial and sympathetic person, but an amusing companion, with a straightforward but graphic sense of humour.

OSBORNE: Hardy says they had a lively time here yesterday. Three big Minnies right in the trench.

TROTTER: I know. And they left the bloomin' 'oles for us to fill in.
(Act I, p. 25/20)

To make Trotter also *look* a figure of fun, however – '*His face is red, fat, and round; apparently he has put on weight during his war service, for his tunic appears to be on the verge of bursting at the waist*' (Act I, p. 22/17) – is a touch which to the modern reader is both inartistic and unnecessary.

There is nothing inartistic or unnecessary about the brash, forced conversation between Stanhope, Trotter and Hibbert in Act III, Scene 2 as they drink excessively not to celebrate the success of the raid on the German lines, but to forget its implications and consequences. The unexpected revelation of Stanhope and Hibbert as purveyors of smutty stories and, probably untrue, amorous escapades serves to enforce the unreality of their poses and to intensify the ghastliness of the situation. And as the scene unfolds towards the inevitable moments of conflict, the enveloping tension is heightened.

Parallels and comparisons in drama and fiction

William Shakespeare: *Henry V*

The links between Laurence Olivier and *Journey's End* and *Henry V* have already been mentioned (pp. 10 and 38), as has the sense of national, and nationalistic, pride and duty which runs through both plays (pp. 37–8). Shakespeare frequently employed battle scenes in his plays, but his lack of concern for dramatic unities of space – he was much more meticulous in his observance of those of time – and the conventions of his age which ignored such niceties as scenery meant that he could readily dispense with any notion of a single setting. Thus characters involved in different incidents and parts of a battle enter and leave the stage at the will and whim of their creator. And while Sherriff shows the prelude to the German assault of 21 March 1918 entirely from within a single dugout in the British trenches, Shakespeare, within one act of *Henry V*, represents the battle of Agincourt on 25 October 1415 by means of seven different imagined settings.

Otherwise, both Shakespeare and Sherriff were faced with a similar dramatic problem of battle conditions. In *Journey's End*, Act III, Scene 1 (pp. 74–5/77–8), a German prisoner needs to be interrogated on stage in such a way that the audience understands what he is saying. Sherriff does this by making both the prisoner and the British Colonel converse in a halting mixture of German and English, a heavy-handed but serviceable device. Shakespeare's solution, in its ultimate employment of an interpreter by an exasperated interrogator, is more elaborate, more realistic, and also more fun. The frightened prisoner is on this occasion French. He has been captured (or more probably discovered) by the disreputable Pistol, who is accompanied by a boy.

PISTOL: Yield, cur!

FRENCH SOLDIER: Je pense que vous êtes gentilhomme de bonne qualité.

PISTOL: Qualitie calmie custure me! Art thou a gentleman? What is thy name? Discuss.

FRENCH SOLDIER: O Seigneur Dieu!

PISTOL: O, Signieur Dew should be a gentleman:
Perpend my words, O Signieur Dew, and mark;
O Signieur Dew, thou diest on point of fox,
Except, O Signieur, thou do give to me
Egregious ransom.

FRENCH SOLDIER: O, prenez miséricorde! Ayez pitié de moi!

PISTOL: Moy shall not serve; I will have forty moys;
Or I will fetch thy rim out at thy throat
In drops of crimson blood.

FRENCH SOLDIER: Est-il impossible d'échapper la force de ton bras?

PISTOL: Brass, cur!
Thou damnèd and luxurious mountain goat,
Offer'st me brass?

FRENCH SOLDIER: O pardonnez moi!

PISTOL: Say'st thou me so? Is that a ton of moys?
Come hither, boy: ask me this slave in French
What is his name.

BOY: Ecoutez: comment êtes-vous appelé?

FRENCH SOLDIER: Monsieur le Fer.

BOY: He says his name is Master Fer.

PISTOL: Master Fer! I'll fer him, and firk him, and ferret him: discuss the same in French unto him.

BOY: I do not know the French for fer, and ferret, and firk . . .

(Act IV, Scene 4)

Sean O'Casey: *The Silver Tassie*

In Sherriff's modest assessment of his initial achievement, quoted above (p. 30), he wrote: '[West End managers] had done their best to get war plays across to the public, and all without exception had failed . . . . All the previous plays had aimed at higher things: they carried "messages", "sermons against war", symbolic revelations.'* All except one of these 'previous plays' are lost in oblivion, but that one, published before the first production of *Journey's End*, but not performed until some months after it, has survived, in spite of, or perhaps even because of, its message and its overt symbolism.

Sean O'Casey (1880–1964) was brought up in a Dublin tenement. Because of an eye disease, he had little education, and taught himself to read. While working as a labourer, he began to write plays. The first three to be produced, *The Shadow of a Gunman* (1923), *Juno and the Paycock* (1924), and *The Plough and the Stars* (1926), proved to be worthy successors of the Irish dramatic movement which had been initiated in particular by the plays of W. B. Yeats (1865–1939) and J. M. Synge (1871–1909), besides reflecting for the first time on the stage the political turbulence and violence, which had torn Ireland apart during the previous decade, and the atmosphere and language of the Dublin slums.

The Silver Tassie begins in the same style and milieu, with Harry Heegan, star and captain of the local football eleven, which has just won the cup (the silver tassie), off to fight in France for the British army. The first act, during which he and his friends celebrate their win and their imminent departure loudly and destructively, ends on an ironic note as his mother, concerned chiefly with the maintenance money she will get, observes: 'Thanks be to Christ that we're after managin' to get the three of them away safely.'† In the second act, the essence rather than the reality of war is expressed in a symbolic setting by anonymous characters representing the exhausted, shattered soldiers, the insensitive high command and vacuous civilian observer, and the perpetually-worked stretcher-bearers with their grim burdens. The horrors and suffering are revealed in clipped dialogue, chants, and repetitions which have the air, and dramatic impulse, of a Greek chorus:

1ST SOLDIER: Cold and wet and tir'd.
2ND SOLDIER: Wet and tir'd and cold.
3RD SOLDIER: Tir'd and cold and wet.
4TH SOLDIER: Twelve blasted hours of ammunition transport fatigue!
1ST SOLDIER: Twelve weary hours.
2ND SOLDIER: And wasting hours.
3RD SOLDIER: And hot and heavy hours.
1ST SOLDIER: Toiling and thinking to build the wall of force that blocks the way from here to home.
2ND SOLDIER: Lifting shells.
3RD SOLDIER: Carrying shells.

No Leading Lady, p. 109.
†*Three More Plays by Sean O'Casey*, Macmillan, London, 1965, p. 46.

4TH SOLDIER: Piling shells.

1ST SOLDIER: In the falling, pissing rine and whistling wind.

2ND SOLDIER: The whistling wind and falling, drenching rain.

3RD SOLDIER: The God-dam rain and blasted whistling wind.*

The act ends in a flurry of disorder and semi-panic which symbolises the misguided reliance on the power of the gun.

STAFF-WALLAH: The enemy has broken through, broken through, broken through!
Every man born of woman to the guns, to the guns.

SOLDIERS: To the guns, to the guns, to the guns!

STAFF-WALLAH: Those at prayer, all in bed, and the swillers drinking deeply in the pubs.

SOLDIERS: To the guns, to the guns.

STAFF-WALLAH: All the batmen, every cook, every bitch's son that hides
A whiff of courage in his veins,
Shelter'd vigour in his body,
That can run, or can walk, even crawl –
Dig him out, dig him out, shove him on –

SOLDIERS: To the guns!

(*The Soldiers hurry to their places led by the Staff-Wallah to the gun. The gun swings around and points to the horizon; a shell is swung into the breech and a flash indicates the firing of the gun, searchlights move over the red glare of the sky; the scene darkens, stabbed with distant flashes and by the more vivid flash of the gun which the Soldiers load and fire with rhythmical movements while the scene is closing. Only flashes are seen; no noise is heard.*)†

O'Casey's impressionistic approach contrasts strongly with Sherriff's realism, though both dramatists were concerned with depicting similar features of the war.

In his third act, however, O'Casey begins to develop his theme of the *effects* of war, returning to the initial style of his first act, though with occasional elusive digressions. Harry, a hero but a hospitalised cripple, loses his girl to his best friend, who has come through unscathed. The silver tassie, symbol of youth and hope, is battered out of shape, and Susie Monican spells out the final message of the play:

. . . We can't give sight to the blind or make the lame walk. We would if we could. It is the misfortune of war. As long as wars are

*Three More Plays, p. 49.
†Three More Plays, pp. 66–7. Compare this extract with Journey's End, Act III, Scene 3, in which the characters, including the cook-batman, go to face the enemy assault in very different order.

waged, we shall be vexed with woe; strong legs shall be made useless and bright eyes made dark. But we, who have come through the fire unharmed, must go on living.*

It is a sign of O'Casey's objectivity as a dramatist that he could extract hope from desperation: and of Sherriff's dedication to the reality which he had witnessed, that he could not do so.

The Silver Tassie had a chequered early history. Raymond Williams could write of it:

The Silver Tassie is a serious experiment in a new form: an extension of naturalism to what is presented as an expressionist crisis. The first and last acts are again the crowded, overflowing talk of the Abbey plays; excited and colourful in its superficial actions – the winning of the cup, the victory dance, the songs – but with a cold using of people, a persistent indifference to each other, that repeats, more bitterly, the paradoxical emotions of the earlier plays . . . . The two middle acts are a newly direct presentation – in their form critically conscious – of the determining suffering . . . . The second act is still one of the most remarkable written in this century . . . . *The Silver Tassie* is memorable and important.†

Yet when O'Casey first submitted it for production at the Abbey Theatre in Dublin, where his other plays had been staged, W. B. Yeats not only rejected it but suggested in his letter to O'Casey:

. . . You are not interested in the Great War; you never stood on its battle fields or walked in its hospitals, and so write out of your own opinions. You illustrate those opinions by a series of almost unrelated scenes, as you might in a leading article: there is no dominating character, no dominating action, neither psychological unity nor unity of action . . . . The mere greatness of the world war has thwarted you; it has refused to become mere background, and obtrudes itself upon the stage as so much dead wood that will not burn with the dramatic fire.‡

O'Casey, in his equally trenchant reply, wrote:

You say – and this is the motif throughout the intonation of your whole song – that 'I am not interested in the Great War'. Now, how do you know I am not interested in the Great War? Perhaps because I never mentioned it to you. Your statement is to me an impudently ignorant one to make, for it happens that I was and am passionately

Three More Plays, pp. 105–6.
†Raymond Williams, *Drama from Ibsen to Brecht*, Penguin Books, London, new edition 1973, pp. 167–8.
‡*The Letters of W. B. Yeats*, edited by Allan Wade, Macmillan, London, 1945, p. 740.

interested in the Great War . . . . You say 'You never stood on its battlefields'. Do you really mean that no one should or could write about or speak about a war because one has not stood on the battle-fields? Were you serious when you dictated that – really serious now? Was Shakespeare at Actium or Philippi?; was G. B. Shaw in the boats with the French, or in the forts with the British when St John and Dunois made the attack that relieved Orleans?*

The upshot was that O'Casey, who had remained in England after a visit in 1926 to receive the Hawthornden Prize, now decided to make his self-imposed exile complete and final. *The Silver Tassie* was first staged in London in 1929, with the American actor Charles Laughton as Harry Heegan, and with a set designed by the painter Augustus John (1878–1961). If there were just one difference between Sean O'Casey's and R. C. Sherriff's visions of the First World War, it *would* be that *The Silver Tassie* could have been, and was, written by someone who had not experienced the trenches at first hand. *Journey's End* could not have been, and its particular success lay in the fact that it was real, and that people recognised it as real.

Oh, What a Lovely War!

Oh, What a Lovely War!, directed by Joan Littlewood, who appro-priately enough was born in 1914, the year in which the First World War began, was first staged in 1963, forty-five years after it ended. This chronicle of the war is presented in the form of a seaside pierrot show of the time and told through contemporary songs and documents against a changing background of slides of news items and photographs of its action. In its impressionistic approach to its depiction of the war and its political background it owed something to *The Silver Tassie* and nothing to *Journey's End*.

SERGEANT: Right, over the top, boys.
    Explosion. They charge and fling themselves on the ground.
    Machine guns.
  Jerry's doin' well.
FIRST SOLDIER: What are all them little yellow flags out there?
SECOND SOLDIER: They give them to our blokes.
FIRST SOLDIER: What for?
SECOND SOLDIER: So they'd know where we was.
SERGEANT: Did you say our blokes?
SECOND SOLDIER: Yea.
FIRST SOLDIER: Oh, I get it, so our guns don't get us before Jerry does.
    Explosion.

*The Letters of W. B. Yeats, p. 115.

SERGEANT: You stick with me, lads. I'll see you through this lot. Heads down and keep spread well out.

SECOND SOLDIER (*sings*): Far far from Wipers I long to be.

SERGEANT: Blimey! You still here?

SECOND SOLDIER: Yeah! Why?

SERGEANT: I drew you in the sweep.

A shell explodes.

I've had enough of this.

SECOND SOLDIER: Me and all.

SERGEANT: Every man for himself.

THIRD SOLDIER: Every man for himself.

SECOND SOLDIER: See you after the war, sarg.

SERGEANT: Yeah, in the Red Lion.

FIRST SOLDIER: Eight o'clock.

SERGEANT: Make it half past.

FIRST SOLDIER: Eh?

SERGEANT: I may be a bit late.*

In its parody of the attitude of the British high command to the fighting on the western front, however, *Oh, What a Lovely War!* would have elicited, and probably did elicit, approval from R. C. Sherriff.

BRITISH GENERAL: Permission to speak, sir? I have been wondering, or rather the staff and I have been wondering, perhaps this policy of attrition might be a mistake. After all, it's wearing us down more than it is them. Couldn't we try a policy of manoeuvre on other fronts?

HAIG: Nonsense. The Western Front is the only real front. We must grind them down. You see, our population is greater than theirs and their losses are greater than ours.

BRITISH GENERAL: I don't quite follow that, sir.

HAIG: In the end they will have five thousand men left and we will have ten thousand and we shall have won. In any case, I intend to launch one more full-scale offensive, and we shall break through and win.

JUNIOR OFFICER (*entering*): I say, sir, did you know that the average life of a young subaltern at the front has now increased to three weeks.

SECOND OFFICER (*entering*): Yes, sir, and replacements are coming in by the thousand; it's marvellous. (*Exit.*)†

Journey's End could only have achieved initial success as a play while the full reality it depicted was still fresh in people's minds. *Oh,*

Oh, What a Lovely War!, Methuen, London, new edition 1967, pp. 90–1.
†*Oh, What a Lovely War!*, pp. 92–3.

What a Lovely War! required a much longer time after the events it parodies before it could be appreciated by a stage audience. Long enough for a forcible and pointed reminder of the tragedy to be salutary: not so long that the historical facts had been generally forgotten.

Willis Hall: *The Long and the Short and the Tall*

As it was after the First World War, a single realistic drama of the Second World War, first produced more than ten years after its end, caught the eye and ear of both critics and audiences at the time and, like *Journey's End*, has not just survived the intervening years but has become a literature text. Willis Hall (*b.*1927) is a Yorkshireman who left school at the age of fifteen and joined the regular army two years later, serving in Singapore and rising to the rank of corporal. When he left the army in 1953 he became a journalist, while also writing plays for radio and television. The play that reached London's West End stage in 1959 as *The Long and the Short and the Tall* had originally been commissioned for presentation at the Edinburgh Festival in 1958, to be performed in the round by a small, all-male, amateur company from Oxford University, some of whose members normally spoke with the regional accents of their places of birth. Hall used his knowledge of the army and of Malaya to write for them a war play, based on the Japanese advance into the peninsula in 1941.

The British theatre of the 1950s had ben revolutionised by the first performance in 1956 of *Look Back in Anger* by John Osborne (*b.*1929), which represented some of the attitudes of and spoke directly to the articulate, educated, lower middle-class generation which had become the theatre's new audience, and Hall's play reflected this new direction. Like *Journey's End*, it has a single set and depicts a group of men under extreme mental pressure and growing physical danger. Its main interest in this context, however, lies in its clearly definable contrasts with *Journey's End*, which emanate from a different set of attitudes to war and to the theatre which had been generated during the intervening thirty years.

Though *The Long and the Short and the Tall* is founded on the realistic situation of a patrol being caught up in and ultimately overrun by the lightning advance of the Japanese forward divisions, the action of the play is entirely fictional, and thus suspense as to the ultimate fate of the men can be maintained in varying degrees throughout it. The effect is heightened by the fact that the action is continuous. Even the period of the statutory interval between the two acts is taken into account in the development of the plot, and has a crucial part to play in the unfolding of the action. There are no officers in the cast list, just a Sergeant (Mitchem), a Corporal, a Lance-Corporal, and four private soldiers. As in *Journey's End*, however, there is an enemy prisoner, a lone Japanese who happens on the deserted hut in the jungle which is the patrol's refuge. The realism with which Sherriff has to contend for purposes of the play in *Journey's End*, Act III, Scene 1, when the Colonel interrogates the German prisoner in a mixture of languages, is brilliantly and much more dramatically projected by Willis Hall in *The Long and the Short and the Tall* in that there is no means of communication between the Japanese and his captors except by signs. The prisoner does not utter a word throughout the play, though he is on stage for almost two-thirds of it. His fate, as Sergeant Mitchem ponders the excruciating choice of taking his prisoner back with them to base and thus risking the lives of all his men, or killing him in cold blood, is the source of further suspense and of conflict between the members of the patrol.

The characters in *Journey's End* tend to be specific types, readily defined and maintaining their basic temperaments throughout the play. While some of the soldiers in *The Long and the Short and the Tall* demonstrate characteristics consistent with their backgrounds and upbringing – there is Bamforth, a sharp, 'streetwise' London Cockney; Lance-Corporal MacLeish, a Scot who displays both the classlessness and the national pride which are justifiably associated with those from his part of Britain; and Smith, a sound, tenacious northerner – there is much greater subtlety in the development of their characters, in their responses to the predicaments with which they are faced, and in the interplay and conflicts between them. For the whole of the first act, the private soldiers, oblivious of any danger in the situation, react as though they are on an exercise. The audience may have similar illusions, and can thus readily respond to the jokes and horseplay, which may be tough and tasteless, but are genuinely meant by those who perpetrate them. As in the one-sided exchange between Bamforth and the Japanese prisoner, to whom he obviously feels protective, on the subject of the latter's wallet:

> BAMFORTH *hands the wallet to* THE PRISONER, *who opens it, extracts a couple of photographs and hands one to* BAMFORTH.
> BAMFORTH: It's a photo! It's a picture of a Nippo bint! (THE PRISONER *points proudly to himself.*) Who's this, then, eh? You got wife? Your missis? (THE PRISONER *points again to himself.*) It's his old woman! Very good. Japanese girl very good, eh? Good old Tojo! She's a bit short in the pins, that's all. But very nice. (THE PRISONER *passes another photograph to* BAMFORTH.) Here! Get this! Nippo snappers, Sarge. Two Jap kids. Couple of chicos. You got two chicos, eh? (THE PRISONER *does not understand.* BAMFORTH *points to the photograph and holds up two fingers.*) Two! See? You got two

kids. (THE PRISONER *shakes his head and holds up three fingers.*) Three? No, you stupid raving imbecile! Two! (BAMFORTH *points again to the photograph.*) One and one's two! Dinky-doo-number-two! (THE PRISONER *holds up his hands to indicate a baby.*) What another? Another one as well! Well, you crafty old devil! You're as bad as Smudge. (BAMFORTH *returns the photographs to* THE PRISONER, *who replaces them carefully in his wallet and returns it to his pocket.*) Let's see if you still know your lessons. Flingers up on blonce! (THE PRISONER *complies.*) Dlop fingers! (*Again* THE PRISONER *is happy to obey.*) Stroll on! See that! He got it right both times! He's almost human this one is!*

There is no reason at this point in the play for the audience to feel any awkwardness about responding to the well-intentioned fun. The humour in *Journey's End*, as we have seen (p. 40), has a specific dramatic purpose, to relieve tension, heighten horror, or momentarily divert attention.

It is, however, in their attitudes to duty and to authority that the two plays differ most. Bamforth can be and is insubordinate to Lance-Corporal MacLeish, and even at the point of supreme crisis defies an order from Sergeant Mitchem, his commander. MacLeish can express doubts about the job he has been called upon to do, as he and Mitchem discuss the prisoner:

MACLEISH: You hear so many stories – you know, on how the Japs treat P.O.W.s.

MITCHEM: Pretty rough, they reckon.

MACLEISH: I'm not so sure. You hear all kinds of things. As if they're almost . . . animals. But this bloke seems a decent sort of bloke.

MITCHEM: It's hard to tell.

MACLEISH: I mean, he's a family man himself.

MITCHEM: So what? Is that supposed to make a difference?

MACLEISH: He's human at least.

MITCHEM: What do you want for your money? Dracula? Look, son, forget the home and family bull. You put a bloke in uniform and push him overseas and he's a different bloke to what he was before. I've watched it happen scores of times.

MACLEISH: But if a bloke's got a wife and family himself . . .

MITCHEM: You get a bloke between your sights and stop to wonder if he's got a family, Jock, your family's not got you. There's half of them got families and most of them are nigs like us who don't know why we're here or what it's all in aid of. It's not your worry. You're not paid to think.

---

*Willis Hall, *The Long and the Short and the Tall*, Heinemann Educational Books, London, 1965, pp. 44–5.

MACLEISH: I used to wonder . . . Worried me a lot . . . I've often wondered, if it came to the push, was it inside me to kill a man.

MITCHEM: It's inside all of us. That's the trouble. Just needs fetching out, some need more to bring it out than others.*

Corporal Johnstone's attitude is different. He is a professional killer, whose hatred for the enemy is in keeping with a certain logic of war which finds no place in *Journey's End*. While Private Smith displays an unquestioning attitude to authority, it is one of resignation, not co-operation: 'I just take orders. I just do as I'm told. I just plod on.'† No heroics for him.

One of the most difficult aspects of *Journey's End* for a modern reader to come to terms with is the natural heroism consistently displayed by its characters. Sergeant Mitchem in *The Long and the Short and the Tall* has some pertinent points to make to MacLeish on the subject of heroism.

MITCHEM: Lad, have you got lots to learn. How did you reckon it was going to be? Like in the comics? Fearless Mac MacLeish charging up a little hill with a score of grenades and highland war cries? Wiping out machine-guns single-handed? The gallant lance-jack gutting half a dozen Nips with a Boy Scout penknife and a Union Jack? Walking back to Jock-land with enough medals to sink a destroyer?

MACLEISH: You're talking through your hat.

MITCHEM (*crossing to* MACLEISH): Yeh? Reckon, do you? Happen so. Perhaps you're right. You happen haven't got the guts for that. I'll tell you this much, boy – a touch like that's the easiest thing on earth. The army's full of square-head yobs who keep their brains between their legs. Blokes who do their nuts for fifteen seconds and cop a decoration, cheer boys cheer, Rule Britannia and death before dishonour. All right. Why not? Good luck to them. Lads like that win wars so they should have the medals. They deserve them. But a touch like this comes harder. The trouble is with war – a lot of it's like this – most of it. Too much. You've got that to learn.‡

The Long and the Short and the Tall is about ordinary men caught up in a situation which they do not fully comprehend and about which they care little. The characters in *Journey's End* care very much about the outward impression they present. They accept the situation and its consequences with such equanimity that the cause for which they are

The Long and the Short and the Tall, pp. 54–5.
†*The Long and the Short and the Tall*, p. 83.
‡*The Long and the Short and the Tall*, p. 61.

fighting needs no elucidation. And that is how it was for them and for the thousands who died in the very circumstances the play projects.

Some novels of the First World War

Four of the more notable novelists of the trenches were respectively a Scot, an Englishman whose father was German-born, an Australian, and a German.

Ian Hay

Ian Hay, pseudonym of John Hay Beith (1876–1952), a grandson of one of the founders of the Free Church of Scotland, was born in Manchester, son of a cotton merchant, and educated at Fettes College, Edinburgh, and St John's College, Cambridge. His first novel, *Pip* (1907), still one of the best novels featuring cricket, became a best-seller, and after two more novels in a similar light vein he gave up being a schoolmaster in 1912 to become a full-time writer. On the outbreak of the First World War he was commissioned in the Argyll and Sutherland Highlanders, serving with them and with the Machine Gun Corps in France from then until 1916, being mentioned in dispatches and awarded the Military Cross. During this time he wrote *The First Hundred Thousand* (1915) and *Carrying On* (1917), before being appointed to the British War Mission in the U.S.A., where he remained for the rest of the war, being made a Commander of the British Empire for his services. After the war he continued his writing career, and also became an adept dramatist. From 1938 to 1941 he was Director of Public Relations at the War Office, with the rank of Major-General.

As novelists and dramatists, and also in that they were both notable oarsmen, Hay and Sherriff had much in common. Both wrote light plays and some even lighter novels. Both reflected the English public-school ethos in writing about the First World War, though Hay neither attended nor taught at one, and Sherriff (as we have seen, pp. 6–7) was considered not to have been at one. Indeed, in Second Lieutenant Bobby Little ('He is a fresh-faced youth, with an engaging smile. Three months ago he was keeping wicket for his school eleven.'*), Hay introduces a young idealist who could be a prototype of Jimmy Raleigh in *Journey's End*. And Hay and Sherriff were writing about the same kind of men undergoing the same kind of experiences, though at different times in the trench-warfare campaign.†

---

*Ian Hay, *The First Hundred Thousand*, Richard Drew, Glasgow, new edition 1985, p. 9.
†At one point in the advance towards Loos in September 1915, described in chapter 21 of *The First Hundred Thousand*, the Argyll and Sutherland Highlanders, in which Hay was

Yet even if one allows for the fact that the technique of the novelist is not the same as that of the dramatist, there is still a clear distinction between the individual voices of Hay and Sherriff, and indeed between Hay and later writers about the First World War.

'When do you think they'll attack?' shouted Bobby to Wagstaffe, battling against the noise of bursting shells.

'Quite soon – in a minute or two. Their guns will stop directly – to lift their sights and set up a barrage behind us. Then, perhaps, the Boche will step over his parapet. Perhaps not!'

The last sentence rang out with uncanny distinctness, for the German guns with one accord had ceased firing. For a full two minutes there was absolute silence, while the bayonets in the opposite trenches twinkled with tenfold intent.

Then, from every point in the great Salient of Ypres, the British guns replied.

Possibly the Great General Staff at Berlin had been misinformed as to the exact strength of the British Artillery. Possibly they had been informed by their Intelligence Department that Trades Unionism had ensured that a thoroughly inadequate supply of shells was to hand in the Salient. Or possibly they had merely decided, after the playful habit of General Staffs, to let the infantry in the trenches take their chance of any retaliation that might be forthcoming.

Whatever these great men were expecting, it is highly improbable that they expected that which arrived. Suddenly the British batteries spoke out, and they all spoke together. In the space of four minutes they deposited *thirty thousand* high-explosive shells in the Boche front-line trenches – yea, distributed the same accurately and evenly along all that crowded arc. Then they paused, as suddenly as they began, while British riflemen and machine-gunners bent to their work.

But few received the order to fire. Here and there a wave of men broke over the German parapet and rolled towards the British lines – only to be rolled back crumpled up by machine guns. Never once was the goal reached. The great Christmas attack was over. After months of weary waiting and foolish recrimination, that exasperating race of bad starters but great stayers, the British people, had delivered 'the goods', and made it possible for their soldiers to speak with the enemy in the gate upon equal – nay, superior, terms.

---

serving, was immediately to the right in the line of the Royal Welch Fusiliers ('that flat-head regiment' – a reference to their caps), with whom was Robert Graves. Graves refers to this in *Good-Bye to All That*, p. 206, though his recollection of the exact wording of Hay's text is faulty.

'Is that all?' asked Bobby Little, peering out over the parapet, a little awestruck at the devastation over the way.*

Perhaps only once, and we should bear in mind that Hay and Sherriff were serving at the front at the same time, but not writing about the same period of the war, do both indulge in the same kind of insouciance. Captain Hardy in *Journey's End*, Act I (p. 10/2), is rather disrespectful to the German trench-weapon known to the British as Minnie. Here is Hay's description.

'Cease fire!' says the major, 'and register!' Then he turns to Captain Blaikie.

'That'll settle them for a bit,' he observes. 'By the way, had any more trouble with Minnie?'

'We had Hades from her yesterday,' replies Blaikie, in answer to this extremely personal question. 'She started at a quarter-past five in the morning, and went on till about ten.'

(Perhaps, at this point, it would be as well to introduce Minnie a little more formally. She is the most unpleasant of her sex, and her full name is *Minenwerfer*, or German trench-mortar. She resides, spasmodically, in Unter den Linden. Her extreme range is about two hundred yards, so she confines her attentions to front-line trenches. Her *modus operandi* is to discharge a large cylindrical bomb into the air. The bomb, which is about fifteen inches long and some eight inches in diameter, describes a leisurely parabola, performing grotesque somersaults on the way, and finally falls with a soft thud into the trench, or against the parapet. There, after an interval of ten seconds, Minnie's offspring explodes; and as she contains about thirty pounds of dynamite, no dug-out or parapet can stand against her.)†

Hay, however, does not avoid the day-to-day realities of war.

Bobby Little, having given the necessary orders to his sergeant, proceeded to [the meeting point] to await the mustering of his platoon.

But the first arrival took the form of a slow-moving procession – a corporal, followed by two men carrying a stretcher. On the stretcher lay something covered with a ground-sheet. At one end projected a pair of regulation boots, very still and rigid.

Bobby caught his breath. He was just nineteen, and this was his first encounter with sudden death.

'Who is it?' he asked unsteadily.

The corporal saluted.

*Ian Hay, *Carrying On*, Blackwood, Edinburgh, 1917, pp. 91–3.
†*The First Hundred Thousand*, pp. 195–6.

'Private McLeary, sirr. That last shot from the trench-mortar got him. It came in kin' o' sideways. He was sittin' at the end of his dug-out, gettin' his tea. Stretcher-party, advance!'

The procession moved off again, and disappeared round the curve.*

Or even more bizarre horrors:

Outside this farm stands a tall tree. Not many months ago a party of Uhlans arrived here, bringing with them a wounded British prisoner. They crucified him to that self-same tree, and stood round him till he died. He was a long time dying.

Some of us had not heard of Uhlans before. These have now noted the name, for future reference – and action.†

These two novels by Hay were written largely at the same time as the events they portray, in a crisp, nonchalant style which reflected the buoyant mood of Britain at the outset of the war. They are totally unlike anything which came later, when the desperation had crept into the war effort, and the disillusionment of hindsight had taken effect on its chroniclers.

Ford Madox Ford

Ford Madox Ford (1873–1939) – he changed his surname from Hueffer in 1919 – was born into a literary family and had his first book, a fairy story called *The Brown Owl*, published in 1892. In all he wrote over eighty books, novels – including two in collaboration with Joseph Conrad (1857–1924) – non-fiction, criticism, and poetry, besides editing the *English Review* and the *Transatlantic Review*. His most lasting individual novel is *The Good Soldier* (1915), a romantic tale of complex passions. *The Fifth Queen* (1906–8) comprises a trilogy of historical novels about Katharine Howard, fifth wife of Henry VIII. Ford was commissioned in the Royal Welch Regiment in 1915, but was invalided home from France in 1917, having been severely gassed.

The novels *Some Do Not* (1924), *No More Parades* (1925), *A Man Could Stand Up* (1926), and *Last Post* (1928) were collected together in 1950 under the title of *Parade's End*. Together they form a semi-autobiographical progress of a Yorkshire squire, Christopher Tietjens, through an unhappy marriage to an agreeable liaison, and safely through the First World War. *A Man Could Stand Up*, in which he serves as an acting commanding officer in the trenches, is thus not so much a war novel in its own right as an integral part of the pattern of its hero's life, the episodes actually in the trenches forming the second of

The First Hundred Thousand, p. 159.
†*The First Hundred Thousand*, p. 149.

the three parts into which the book is divided. It is nevertheless interesting in the context of these Notes in that, like *Journey's End*, it was written some time after the events it purports to describe, and thus from a considered viewpoint. Ford's attitude to his non-commissioned officers and private soldiers is similar to Sherriff's, too, in that they are usually presented as ciphers (as is the Sergeant-Major in *Journey's End*) or as excuses for humour (as is Sherriff's cook-batman), and he indulges in copious phonetic dialect to represent their speech.

Because a novelist is, by the nature of his craft, able to give a broader picture than the dramatist, and to tell in immediate, descriptive prose what can only be hinted at on the stage, Ford offers some significant sidelights.

> That had been in, presumably, February, and, presumably, it was now April. The way the dawn came up looked like April . . . . What did it matter? . . . That damned truck had stayed under that bridge for two hours and a half . . . in the process of the eternal waiting that is War. You hung about, and you kicked your heels and you kicked your heels: waiting for Mills bombs to come, or for jam, or for generals, or for the tanks, or transport, or the clearance of the road ahead. You waited in offices under the eyes of somnolent orderlies, under fire on the banks of canals, you waited in hotels, dug-outs, tin sheds, ruined houses. There will be no man who survives of His Majesty's Armed Forces, that shall not remember those eternal hours when Time itself stayed still as the true image of bloody War!*

He also has some very telling things to say about the nature of command, which features as a discussion point so frequently in *Journey's End*.

> Tietjens had a very great respect for the abilities of the Commanding Officer as Commanding Officer. His rag-time battalion of a rag-time army was as nearly on the level of an impeccable regular battalion as such a unit with its constantly changing personnel could possibly be . . . . It was a very great achievement to have got men to fire at moments of such stress with such complete tranquility. For discipline works in two ways: in the first place it enables the soldier in action to get through his movements in the shortest possible time; and then the engrossment in the exact performance begets a great indifference to danger. When, with various sized pieces of metal flying all round you, you go composedly through efficient bodily movements, you are not only wrapped up in your task, but you have the knowledge that the exact performance is every minute decreasing your personal danger. In addition you have the feeling

---

The Bodley Head Ford Madox Ford, Volume IV, 1963, p. 342.

that Providence ought to – and very frequently does – specially protect you.*

Frederic Manning

Frederic Manning (1882–1935) was born in Australia, a younger son of a four-times Lord Mayor of Sydney, and educated at Sydney Grammar School. A chronic asthmatic, he came to live in England in 1898. He published poetry and short stories, and from 1909 to 1914 reviewed books for the *Spectator*. In October 1914 he joined the King's Shropshire Light Infantry as a private, and fought on the Somme. He later became an officer in the Royal Irish Regiment, was arrested for insubordination, and diagnosed as suffering from shell-shock. His war novel, which he was finally pushed into writing by his publisher, was first published in 1929 in a limited edition as *The Middle Parts of Fortune*, and only subsequently under the title by which it is now known, *Her Privates We*.

The novel was thus subconsciously gestating for about as long as *Journey's End*. In a prefatory note to his book, Manning wrote:

> While the following pages are a record of experience on the Somme and Ancre fronts . . . and the events in it actually happened; the characters are fictitious. It is true that in recording the conversations of the men I seemed at times to hear the voices of ghosts . . . . I have drawn no portraits; and my concern has been mainly with the anonymous ranks, whose opinion, often mere surmise and ill-informed, but real and true for them, I have tried to represent faithfully.†

In being written by someone who was at the time an ordinary soldier, and representing the point of view of the ordinary soldier, *Her Privates We* differs from *Journey's End* and from any novel or auto-biographical work published in the dozen or so years after the end of the First World War, even if Bourne, its main character, who clearly has affinities with Manning himself, is an unusual private, well-educated and something of a philosopher, as well as an adept scrounger of comforts. The period of the war about which he was writing, the latter half of 1916, was just about when the cheerful optimism expressed in Hay's novels was beginning to give way to disillusionment, which in its turn was ultimately affected by the kind of hopeless resignation which sometimes surfaces in *Journey's End*.

> Mr Finch was standing only a few feet away, and he glanced at the boy talking to Bourne, looked after him as he turned and ran, and

The Bodley Head Ford Madox Ford, Volume IV, pp. 356–7.
†Frederic Manning, *Her Privates We*, Hogarth Press, London, new edition 1986, p. xi.

then turned to Bourne himself.

'Seems a bloody shame to send a kid like that into a show, doesn't it?' he said, in a kindly undertone.

'He was with us on the Somme, in July and August, sir,' was all Bourne's reply, though that he, too, thought it a bloody shame was sufficiently obvious.

'Was he?' exclaimed Mr Finch appreciatively. 'Stout fellow. It's a bloody shame, all the same.'

He struck at a clod of mud with his stick.

'Bloody awful weather to go over in, isn't it?' he said, almost as though he were only thinking aloud. 'However, we can only do our best.'*

Unlike the characters in *Journey's End*, however, those in *Her Privates We* express, as well as feel, fear.

Bourne's fit of shakiness increased, until he set his teeth to prevent them chattering in his head; and after a deep, gasping breath, almost like a sob, he seemed to recover to some extent. Fear poisoned the very blood; but, when one recognized the symptoms, it became objective, and one seemed to escape partly from it that way . . . . Some men moaned, or even sobbed a little, but unconsciously, and as though they struggled to throw off an intolerable burden of oppression. His eyes met Shem's, and they both turned away at once from the dread and question which confronted them.†

And also hatred:

Again he heard some rifle-fire, some bombing, and, stooping, he ran towards the sound, and was by Minton's side again, when three men ran towards them, holding their hands up and screaming; and he lifted his rifle to his shoulder and fired; and the ache in him became a consuming hate that filled him with exultant cruelty, and he fired again, and again.‡

But the hatred which follows the death of the young lad who is his friend is replaced by a state of shock which recalls that of Raleigh after the loss of Osborne in *Journey's End*, Act III, Scene 2.

'You don't want to think o' things,' [Sergeant Tozer] said, with brutal kindness. 'It's all past an' done wi', now.'

Bourne looked at him in a dull acquiescence. Then he emptied the tin, replaced it on the bench, and, getting up, went to sit by the door again. He sat with his head flung back gainst the earth, his eyes

Her Privates We, pp. 205–6.
†*Her Privates We*, p. 212.
‡*Her Privates We*, p. 217.

closed, his arms relaxed, and his hands idle in his lap, and he felt as though he were lifting a body in his arms, and looking at a small impish face, the brows puckered with a shadow of perplexity, bloody from a wound in the temple, the back of the head almost blown away; and yet the face was quiet, and unmoved by trouble. He sat there for hours, immobile and indifferent, unaware that Sergeant Tozer glanced at him occasionally. The shelling gradually died away, and he did not know it.*

Erich Maria Remarque

'*Im Westen nichts Neues*' ('No news in the West') was how the German newspapers shrugged off the fact that by the high summer of 1918 a whole generation of men on their western front was being shelled, bombed, shot, or gassed to death, and that those who survived would never get over the experience. One of these young men was Erich Maria Remarque (1898–1970), who took those words as the ironical title of his novel, published in Germany in January 1929, the very month in which *Journey's End* opened on the West End stage in London, and in England (under the title of *All Quiet on the Western Front*) two months later. Like *Journey's End*, it was an immediate sensation, and sold two-and-a-half million copies world wide within eighteen months. In 1932 Remarque left Germany in disillusionment at the Nazi regime. In 1933 his book was officially banned in Germany and copies of it symbolically burned for its 'defeatist' attitude, along with many books by Jewish and other writers, the existence of which was said to be undermining the state. In 1937 he went to the U.S.A., where he published a number of novels in English. He became an American citizen in 1947.

In that it is written in the first person, and in the present tense, *All Quiet on the Western Front* reads in parts more like an autobiography than a novel, but there is an inexorable pattern about the way the group of friends from the same school meet their dreadful ends, along with their colleagues in the company in which they are serving. The period of the war which it describes is the last summer, shortly after the events of *Journey's End*, when the British and their allies were taking the final initiative. If it has affinities with any of the other books discussed here, however, it is with *Her Privates We*, in that it is entirely about ordinary soldiers. There is the same uneasy distinction between action at the front and behind the lines, and the same preoccupation with lice, rats, mud, and scrounging for food and comforts. But it is a more horrific book than any of them, and asks more questions of its readers.

*_Her Privates We_, pp. 220–1.

'But what I would like to know,' says Albert, 'is whether there would have been a war if the Kaiser had said No.'

'I'm sure there would,' I interject, 'he was against it from the first.'

'Well, if not him alone, then perhaps if twenty or thirty people in the world said No.'

'That's probable,' I agree, 'but they damned well said Yes.'

'It's queer, when one thinks about it,' goes on Kropp, 'we are here to protect our fatherland. And the French are over there to protect their fatherland. Now who's in the right?'

'Perhaps both,' I say without believing it.

'Yes, well now,' pursues Albert, and I see that he means to drive me into a corner, 'but our professors and parsons and newspapers say that we are the only ones that are right, and let's hope so; – but the French professors and parsons and newspapers say that right is on their side, now what about that? . . .'

Tjaden reappears. He is still quite excited and again joins the conversation, wondering how a war gets started.

'Mostly by one country badly offending another,' answers Albert with a slight air of superiority.

Then Tjaden pretends to be obtuse. 'A country? I don't follow. A mountain in Germany cannot offend a mountain in France. Or a river, or a wood, or a field of wheat.'

'Are you really as stupid as that, or are you just pulling my leg?' growls Kropp, 'I don't mean that at all. One people offends the other –'

'Then I haven't any business here at all,' replies Tjaden, 'I don't feel myself offended.'*

Perhaps with more questioning of this kind on the part of young people, the terrible sacrifices of the two world wars in terms of innocent civilians as well as service personnel may not be repeated. The plays, autobiographical accounts, and novels which have lived on and been continually reprinted are salutary reminders as well as literary records.

---

*Erich Maria Remarque, *All Quiet on the Western Front* (translated by A. W. Wheen), Pan Books, London, new edition 1987, pp. 134–5.

Part 4

Hints for study

PLAYS ARE WRITTEN to be performed. The stage directions and sound effects (which are particularly significant in *Journey's End*), even the silences, as well as the dialogue, together make up the total exposition which the audience sees and hears. Serious readers of the play script – for that is what in this case it is – must exercise imagination if the author's intentions are to be understood and appreciated. Sherriff's stage directions are very precise, as are his descriptions even of his minor characters. As you read the play, try in your mind to see it and hear it in the same way as an audience would. Passages of dialogue which may at first sight seem to be about nothing in particular should now assume greater significance and purpose. When played on the stage, the desultory and sometimes inconsequential conversation between Osborne and Raleigh in Act II, Scene 1, for instance, contributes considerably to the building up and drawing out of the tension before the raid, which itself is depicted in terms of sound only.

Journey's End is not a complex play, but that does not mean that questions on it can be answered without knowing the play, and the people in it, in detail. A familiarity with one or more other war plays, and with novels or autobiographies of the trenches will pay dividends. There is also a whole body of poetry of the First World War which adds an extra dimension to its literature.

Here are three sample questions.

---

(1) George Bernard Shaw, in a letter to R. C. Sherriff, who had asked for an opinion on the manuscript of *Journey's End*, stated: 'This play is, properly speaking, a document, not a drama'.* Discuss this criticism.

Shaw was himself a dramatist, as well as a theatre critic, and during the 1890s and early years of the twentieth century he sought to recall drama to ways of realism with such plays as *Mrs Warren's Profession*, *The Doctor's Dilemma*, and *Major Barbara*. He was also, however, a consummate artist who could, and did, invest his plays with wit, social satire, and theatrical devices, besides making them platforms for the discussion of ideas. To us today, brought up on television 'docudrama' (the dramatised representation of real people reacting to real

*Quoted in *No Leading Lady*, p. 45.

situations and events) and on 'faction' (the employment of the medium of the novel to similar ends), it could be said to be even easier to appreciate what he meant by his statement about *Journey's End*, and why he made it. *Journey's End* has as its background a real situation and is peopled by men whom Sherriff claims in his autobiography, *No Leading Lady* (1968), he knew, speaking as they spoke. Certainly, too, the recurring conversation about the meals they are eating, however much it is an added touch of realism, is not what one usually associates with dramatic dialogue. The characters of the main protagonists are established from their first entrance, and there is little or no development in any of them to intrigue the audience in that particular dramatic aspect, nor is any of them ever faced with a choice of actions, while the play's end, with its implications of failure and of total destruction, resolves none of the problems inherent in or stemming from the basic situation from which the action of the play embarks.

It is, however, when we examine other aspects of the play that characteristics of genuine drama emerge – the presentation and development of theme, the handling of suspense and tension, and the introduction of personal conflicts which heighten that tension. The original theme of the play, we learn from *No Leading Lady*, was the hero-worship of young Jimmy Raleigh, into the trenches straight from school, for the older Dennis Stanhope, who is also, as we understand from the conversation between Raleigh and Osborne, and between Osborne and Stanhope, in Act I, likely to become his brother-in-law. Stanhope's fear that Raleigh will reveal to Madge the changes that have been wrought in him by his continuous service at the front is the source of conflict between them. The very different kind of hero that Stanhope has become, of whose attributes Raleigh quickly becomes aware, is not the sort of person Stanhope wants to appear to his intended fiancée. To Raleigh, the only chink in the perfection of the changed Stanhope is his apparent insensitivity after the death of Osborne in the raid on the German line which takes place in Act III, Scene 1. But Stanhope, the true commanding officer, is only hiding his enormous grief at the loss of his confidant and friend so as not to upset his officers and men. There is a dramatic moment of truth when this is revealed to Raleigh. Yet, in another dramatic twist, when the final moment of understanding comes between them, after Raleigh has been brought down into the dugout to die, it is too late for either of them. The misunderstandings which are at the heart of the personal conflict, then, represent a considerable exercise in dramatic irony.

Besides hero-worship, there is an inherent theme of heroism itself, displayed by the characters in different ways: by Raleigh, with the unquestioning faith of his youth; by Osborne, with the thoughtfulness that comes from his age and experience; by Trotter, with his unimaginative cheerfulness; by Stanhope and the Sergeant-Major, as they unconcernedly discuss the inevitable destruction of the Company; and even by Hibbert, at his final exit, unwilling to be seen by the kindly cook-batman to be afraid.

There is suspense even in Act I as, having received two apparently conflicting views, from Captain Hardy and from Osborne, about Stanhope's fitness for command, the audience awaits his entrance, to form their own conclusions. It recurs in Act II, Scene 2 as we await the outcome of the confrontation between Stanhope and Hibbert. It is in the halting conversation between Osborne and Raleigh in Act III, Scene 1 as they await the time for the raid, followed by the almost unbearable tension until the fate of its members is revealed, cleverly delayed for the utmost effect until after the by-play of the interrogation by the Colonel of the German prisoner. And suspense runs through the final scene of the play as the characters, each in his own way, prepare for their fate.

Martin Esslin wrote in *An Anatomy of Drama*: 'Drama is not only the most concrete – that is, the least abstract – artistic imitation of real human behaviour, it is also the most concrete form in which we can think about human situations.'* The passage of years since *Journey's End* was written has served to heighten rather than diminish its significance to an audience as a means of assimilating real human behaviour and of exploring the historical situation which motivated it. In these terms, though *Journey's End* may not be a great piece of literature, or even an outstanding play, it is certainly more than mere documentary.

---

(2) Discuss the significance of the minor characters in *Journey's End*: Captain Hardy; the Colonel; the Sergeant-Major; Mason.

The five principal characters in the play are each represented as a particular type of person. Stanhope, schoolboy hero to Raleigh and battle hero to his officers and men, has suffered the inevitable effects of continuous service, and command, at the front. Osborne is the archetypal middle-aged public school master, dependable and philosophical. Trotter is much as the middle-class audiences of the 1920s and 1930s might view a likeable and effective officer from a working-class background, rather as a figure of fun. Hibbert is, by comparison with his fellow officers, a weakling and a coward. Raleigh is a starry-eyed lad straight from school. Each of the four minor characters has a part to play in increasing our knowledge of the main characters or of the situation, and in the development of the action.

*Martin Esslin, *An Anatomy of Drama*, Sphere Books, London, new edition 1976, p. 21.

Captain Hardy, commander of the Company which is being relieved by C Company, only appears at the very beginning of the play, and is by contrast with Stanhope and Osborne disorganised as well as overtly cheerful. He is more concerned with eliciting what comfort and amusement he can from the situation and with getting out of it as quickly as possible, than with making proper transfer of command or even with the well-being of his men – he appears neither to care nor even to know where or how his men sleep when off duty. Through his attitude and demeanour the greater effectiveness of the C Company command is fully illustrated at the outset of the play. The conversation between Hardy and Osborne has a further purpose, however, which is to offer the audience two utterly contrasting views of Stanhope. To Hardy, he is a likeable enough person but an unworthy commanding officer with a severe drink problem. Through Osborne's replies and responses we get a different, fuller, and more plausible picture of a brilliant man whose nerves have been shattered by continuous service at the front but whose qualities of leadership and ability to command the loyalty of his officers and men are in no doubt. Thus the background to the major character in the play is teased out and established, while the audience's interest is heightened in anticipation of his first entrance.

The Colonel of the Regiment of which C Company is a part is answerable to the unseen Brigadier, but represents the high command whose efficacy and tactics at the time were and have been ever since called into question. He is bluff, unsure of himself when giving Stanhope the initial instructions about the raid in Act II, Scene 2 and immediately after it (he is unwilling that Stanhope should leave him to go and see to his men), and so insensitive to the fate of the participants in the raid that he only remembers to ask about them as an afterthought. He is not so much an object of fun or contempt as one of satire, and he elicits from Stanhope the only expression of disillusionment in the play. In Act III, Scene 1 the Colonel tries to restore his credibility as the officer ultimately responsible for the raid by expressing belated regret at the loss of Osborne. Stanhope replies: 'Still it'll be awfully nice if the brigadier's pleased.'

The Company Sergeant-Major is both the physical and the symbolic embodiment of the ordinary soldiers in C Company. He is also the official link between them and their commander, and through his conversation with Stanhope in Act II, Scene 2 the full implications become apparent to the audience of the situation the Company will be in when the assault comes. He is a large man (for the purposes of the play he has to carry the dying Raleigh down the steps into the dugout in Act III, Scene 3) whose presence obviously terrifies the German prisoner in Act III, Scene 1. He is also, by contrast with the traditional view that is held of his like, a kindly man, as his subsequent treatment of the prisoner reveals, with a wry sense of humour. He demonstrates this when responding to Stanhope's answer to his question in Act II, Scene 2:

S-M (*diffidently*): Yes, sir, but what 'appens when the Boche 'as all got round the back of us?

STANHOPE: Then we advance and win the war.

S-M (*pretending to make a note*): Win the war. Very good, sir.

Sherriff expended similar care in his delineation of the character of Mason, the cook-batman. According to Sherriff's recollection of the broadcast by the influential critic, James Agate, after the Stage Society's first production of *Journey's End* in December 1928, from which he quotes in his autobiography, *No Leading Lady* (1968), every appearance of Mason 'brought the house down'. Much of the genuine humour in the play centres on the quick responses between him and the officers about the food he serves to them, in which even Stanhope joins when they are discussing in Act II, Scene 2 the curious taste of the tea.

STANHOPE: In other words, it's onion soup with tea-leaves in it?

MASON: Not till dinner-time, sir.

STANHOPE: All right, Mason. Bring two cups of onion tea. One for Mr Hibbert.

When officers off duty met together for a brief meal, that and food in general was not only the safest and easiest topic to take their minds off their situation, but also one in which they could all participate. Mason is the means whereby the realism of the conversation is enlivened, and humour introduced into the dialogue as a means of temporarily relieving the dramatic tension which is never far from the audience's consciousness throughout the play. The way Mason makes his last exit, displaying a touch of genuine humanity and diplomacy in asking to accompany the terrified Hibbert to his post ('I'd like to come along of you if you don't mind, sir. I ain't bin up in this part of the front line. Don't want to get lorst.') is one of the most poignant moments in the play.

---

(3) Does the play of *Journey's End* offer any messages to those who strive for world peace?

R. C. Sherriff, in his autobiography, *No Leading Lady* (1968), expressed his surprise that his play should have been taken up for its first public performance by Maurice Browne, who was a confirmed pacifist and conscientious objector, and had stayed in the U.S.A. for the duration of the First World War. His surprise might appear to be justified in that throughout the play no character expresses any revulsion or distaste for war, nor questions the reasons why they are in such an unpleasant and ultimately impossible situation, or the orders which have put them there. It is sometimes said that war provides a release for the belligerent attitudes of its instigators and its combatants. If such a trait were demonstrated by any of the characters in *Journey's End*, as it is, for instance, by Corporal Johnstone in Willis Hall's play of the Second World War, *The Long and the Short and the Tall* (1959), then that might suggest that its author was introducing an argument against war. Yet so far from any of the characters being in any way depicted as aggressive, none of them even displays any hatred towards their enemy. On the contrary, in Act II, Scene 1, Osborne gives Raleigh an example of humanity and decency on the part of a German officer who allowed a wounded man to be retrieved from No Man's Land, an incident which has a real life counterpart in Robert Graves's autobiography, *Good-Bye to All That* (1929). The characters in *Journey's End*, men as well as officers, are represented as ordinary people from varying backgrounds, all of them kindly, and working together under a commander they respect towards a common goal, loyal to each other and to their duty. War is certainly not depicted as glorious, but heroism is to be admired, and rewarded.

Yet these aspects of the characters and their actions can be seen in a different light. Unquestioning obedience to duty and to orders is a necessary attribute for a soldier in situations in which a split second can mean the difference between life and death. You cannot have a committee meeting to discuss every decision, even at the highest level. The conduct of war, as the play illustrates, is autocratic, not democratic, and men are expected to die in obedience to orders for causes of which they have little understanding and even less concern. This is nowhere explicitly stated in *Journey's End*, as it is, for instance, in Erich Maria Remarque's novel, *All Quiet on the Western Front* (1929), but it is inherent by implication. To go out and kill your enemies, for whom you have no hatred, fortified just by a small tot of rum, requires a conditioning of the mind to exclude feelings of humanity, or else a mind which has been artificially conditioned. These are attributes which are destructive to society as well as, in conditions of war, to life.

Journey's End, because it is dealing with ordinary people in extra-ordinary situations – for none of the officers of C Company is a professional soldier – illustrates clearly the effects of war in breaking up people's lives and changing their personalities. We are led to understand that if they had survived, only perhaps the older Osborne, with his innate toughness of body and mind and pattern of life already established, might have been able to pick up the pieces of his former existence. The others, even Trotter, will have lost their most formative years.

Sherriff was writing for an audience of whom many had personally experienced the war in different forms, and others were even now beginning to see a subsequent world war as a likely corollary of political, social, and economic conditions in Germany. To these people, war was still an unfortunate, undesirable condition of life in those times. The new generations in the English-speaking world, to whom Korea and Vietnam are history, and even the Falklands campaign of 1982, fought by professional servicemen, so far away geographically as to be difficult to comprehend, are growing up with no experience of fighting a war, or of a war being fought by their lovers, friends, and relations. To them in particular, *Journey's End* offers a frightening and salutary picture of ordinary people, with initially no inclination or training for fighting, being called upon by the circumstances of their birth to perform the most distasteful duty of all under the most appalling conditions imaginable. In these respects, by the very reason of its reality, *Journey's End* has come to offer powerful pacifist arguments.

Part 5

Suggestions for further reading

The text

Journey's End, acting edition, Samuel French, London, 1931.
Journey's End, with introduction and notes by E. R. Wood, Heinemann Educational Books, London, 1958.
Journey's End, Penguin Books, London, 1983.

Some other books and plays by R. C. Sherriff

The Fortnight in September, Gollancz, London, 1931 (novel).
Home at Seven, Samuel French, London, 1950 (play).
Journey's End, Gollancz, London, 1930 (novel).
The Long Sunset, Samuel French, London, 1958 (play).
No Leading Lady, Gollancz, London, 1968 (autobiography).
The Wells of St Mary's, new edition, Pan Books, London, 1963 (novel).

Some other war plays

HALL, WILLIS: *The Long and the Short and the Tall*, Heinemann Educational Books, London, 1965.
LITTLEWOOD, JOAN (PRODUCER): *Oh, What a Lovely War!*, Methuen, London, 1965.
O'CASEY, SEAN: *The Silver Tassie*, in *Three More Plays by Sean O'Casey*, Macmillan, London and Basingstoke, 1965.

Some literature of the First World War

BLUNDEN, EDMUND: *Undertones of War*, new edition, Penguin Books, London, 1984 (autobiography).
CROSS, TIM (ED.): *The Lost Voices of World War I*, Bloomsbury, London, 1988 (anthology of prose, verse, and drama).
FORD, FORD MADOX: *A Man Could Stand Up*, in *The Bodley Head Ford Madox Ford*, Volume IV, Bodley Head, London, 1963 (novel).
GIDDINGS, ROBERT (ED.): *The War Poets*, Bloomsbury, London, 1988 (anthology).

GRAVES, ROBERT: *Good-Bye to All That*, new edition, Penguin Books, London, 1969 (autobiography).

HAY, IAN: *The First Hundred Thousand*, new edition, Richard Drew, Glasgow, 1985 (novel).

HAY, IAN: *Carrying On*, Blackwood, Edinburgh, 1917 (novel).

MANNING, FREDERIC: *Her Privates We*, new edition, Hogarth Press, London, 1986 (novel).

REMARQUE, ERICH MARIA: *All Quiet on the Western Front*, (translated by A. W. Wheen), new edition, Pan Books (Picador Classics), London, 1987 (novel).

SASSOON, SIEGFRIED: *Memoirs of an Infantry Officer*, new edition, Faber, London, 1965 (autobiography).

SILKIN, JON (ED.): *The Penguin Book of First World War Poetry*, 2nd edition, Penguin Books, London, 1981.

STEPHEN, MARTIN: *Never Such Innocence: a New Anthology of Great War Verse*, Buchan & Enright, Tolworth, Surrey, 1988.

Background reading

DUNN, Captain J. C.: *The War the Infantry Knew 1914–1918: a Chronicle of Service in France and Belgium with the Second Battalion His Majesty's Twenty-Third Foot, The Royal Welch Fusiliers*, new edition, Sphere Books, London, 1989.

ESSLIN, MARTIN: *An Anatomy of Drama*, new edition, Sphere Books, London, 1978.

FUSSELL, PAUL: *The Great War and Modern Memory*, Oxford University Press, New York, 1975 (critical study of the literature of the First World War, especially as it reflects life in the trenches).

KEEGAN, JOHN: *The Face of Battle*, new edition, Penguin Books, London, 1978.

MACDONALD, LYN (ED.): *1914–1918: Voices and Images of the Great War*, Michael Joseph, London, 1988.

MACDONALD, LYN: *The Roses of No Man's Land*, new edition, Macmillan, London and Basingstoke, 1984.

MACQUEEN POPE, W.: *The Footlights Flickered*, Herbert Jenkins, London, 1959.

TREWIN, J. C.: *Dramatists of Today*, Staples Press, London, 1953.

WOLFF, LEON: *In Flanders Fields*, new edition, Penguin Books, London, 1979.

The author of these notes

ANTONY KAMM, whose father served in France during the First World War, was born in London and educated at Charterhouse and Worcester College, Oxford, where he read Classics and then English Language and Literature and was President of the Oxford University English Society. He has held senior editorial posts with several leading publishers, most recently Oxford University Press. He was a Senior Education Officer, Commonwealth Secretariat, from 1972 to 1974, and he has on several occasions been a consultant to Unesco and other international organisations on the provision and production of books. He is at present a part-time lecturer in the Department of English Studies, University of Stirling. His publications include *The Story of Islam*, York Notes on *The Long and the Short and the Tall*, the York Handbook *A Dictionary of British and Irish Authors*, and the anthologies *The Scottish Collection of Verse to 1800* (with Eileen Dunlop), and *An Irish Childhood* and *A Jewish Childhood* (with A. N. Jeffares).